MW00576833

DESPONDENCY

The Spiritual Teaching of Evagrius Ponticus on Acedia

Despondency

The Spiritual Teaching of Evagrius Ponticus on Acedia

GABRIEL BUNGE

translated from the German by
ANTHONY P. GYTHIEL

ST VLADIMIR'S SEMINARY PRESS
YONKERS, NEW YORK
2012

Library of Congress Cataloging-in-Publication Data

Bunge, Gabriel, 1940–
    [Akedia. English]
    Despondency : the spiritual teaching of Evagrius Ponticus on acedia /
Gabriel Bunge ; translated from the German by Anthony P. Gythiel.
        p. cm.
    Includes bibliographical references and index.
    ISBN 978-0-88141-394-6 (alk. paper)
        1. Evagrius, Ponticus, 345?–399. 2. Acedia—History of Doctrines—Early church,
ca. 30–600. 3. Spirituality—History—Early church, ca. 30–600. I. Title.
    BR1720.E9B8613 2011
    241'.3—dc23

                                                                    2011040934

Translation copyright © 2011

ST VLADIMIR'S SEMINARY PRESS
575 Scarsdale Rd, Yonkers, NY 10707
1-800-204-2665
www.svspress.com

A translation of Gabriel Bunge, *Akēdia*
Die geistliche Lehre des Evagrios Pontikos vom Überdruss.
Würzburg, Verlag « Der Christliche Osten. »

ISBN 978-0-88141-394-6

Confitebor tibi in cithara, Deus, Deus meus.

Quare tristis es anima mea et quare conturbas

me? Spera in Deum quoniam adhuc confitebor

illi, salutare vultus mei et Deus meus.

I will praise the Lord my God with the harp.

Why are you filled with sadness, my soul? Why

are you so distraught? Trust in God for I shall

give praise to him. He is the one who saves me,

the light of my eyes, and my God.

Ps 42 (43):4–5

Table of Contents

Preface   9

Introduction:
   Evagrius as Spiritual Teacher   11

1. *Acedia—A Disease Typical only of Monks?*   21

2. *The Definition of Evil*   37

3. *The Origin and Characteristics of Vice*   51

4. *Manifestations of Despondency*   65

5. *The Remedies*   87

6. *Acedia and the Spiritual Life*   117

Epilogue   133

Works by Evagrius   141

Other Source Texts   145

Other Evagriana by the Author   146

General Index (Names & Topics)   149

Preface

In 1983, when this little book appeared for the first time in the book trade in a series[1] of the late Wilhelm Nyssen, and one that was difficult to obtain, I would never have thought it possible that after a little more than ten years, I would have to prepare the work for a fourth edition. Meanwhile, the first, second (a reprinting) and the following editions, available in the regular book trade, went out of print rather quickly. People to whom this modest volume was apparently useful, must have passed on the title to one another like a "secret tip" (W. Nyssen).

Neither then nor today did I pursue scientific ambitions with this investigation. It was, and simply is, a matter of making available to others the "wisdom of the Fathers" whose living power I had experienced myself and still perceive daily. The theme itself—spiritual despondency —has already been dealt with by many others, even in comprehensive monographs, right up to the very recent past; most of this material is known to me. Nevertheless, faithful to my original intention, in this most recent edition as well I have decided against imparting to the whole a "scientific" appearance.

After more than twenty years, an author has the entirely natural feeling that he would actually formulate the text differently today. Nevertheless, I have resisted the temptation of an entirely new version, and this time I have restricted myself to expressing the thought more precisely here and there, to correcting obvious errors and improving the translation of patristic texts by using the most recent critical editions and, eventually, to adding a few additional "pearls."

The readers, for whom, as for the author, it is above all a matter of *deepening the spiritual life*, will endure the still remaining imper-

---

[1] W. Nyssen, ed., Schriftenreihe des Zentrums patristischer Spiritualität Koinonia-Oriens im Erzbistum Köln, vol. 9 (Cologne, 1983).

fections with patience—the Evagrian cure-all against despondency. For this, the author offers his sincere thanks.

Hieroschemamonk Gabriel Bunge
Hermitage of the Holy Cross

Evagrius as Spiritual Teacher

E arly monasticism produced an abundance of interesting and original figures, beginning with Antony the Great, "the first of the anchorites,"[1] whose biography, for the first time, made Egyptian monasticism known to an astonished world. Among these "desert fathers," Evagrius Ponticus (*c.* 345–399),[2] whom we have selected here as our teacher, occupies an exceptional place in many respects.

Considered purely chronologically, Evagrius belongs already to the third generation of anchorites: his own teacher, Macarius the Great, had known Antony. Evagrius thus had a "tradition" ready at his disposal, one that was pure and unadulterated, to go along with his own rich experience. In addition to Macarius the Great, it was above all Macarius' namesake, Macarius of Alexandria, who introduced Evagrius into the monastic life. Evagrius himself was certainly an unusual personality, a monk and a theologian all in one. For a desert father, he was also a prolific writer, perhaps the first who adhered so closely in writing to the desert wisdom. Let us briefly outline his life circumstances, as they throw a bright light on his spiritual teaching.

Only the *Lausiac History* of Palladius stands at our disposal as a full biographical source, since Evagrius in his own writings was extremely reserved about his own person. A long-time disciple, friend, and confidant of Evagrius, Palladius is undoubtedly a trustworthy guide. Nonetheless, some suspicion is well-founded, in that his work has not come down to us in its original form.[3] Numerous

[1]*M.* c. 35.
[2]For person and life, see G. Bunge, *Briefe, Einleitung* (Introduction) A.
[3]See G. Bunge, "*Palladiana* I. Introduction aux fragments coptes de l'Histoire Lausiaque," *Studia Monastica* 32 (1990), 79–129 (81ff.; "Evagrius and his friends in the Lausiac History").

patently tendentious variants in the Greek manuscripts tell us that the text has passed through many hands, including some that were not always well disposed towards Evagrius and his friends. Thus, some important names and details having to do with Evagrius and his circle are concealed in alternative readings, preserved in the footnotes of the critical text, from which they may be lifted with care.

Beyond Palladius, a longer, more detailed version of the *Vita* of Evagrius—preserved today in a large fragment in Greek and a few allusions in a Coptic translation—raises the fundamental question whether the well-known Greek text is altogether a later "purified" abridged version from a first *Vita Evagrii* from the pen of Palladius.

In a sense, the biography of Evagrius shares the same fate as his works: much has been lost or has come down to us only in fragments; some is preserved under a false name and has been restored to him only recently; the greater part is accessible only in a Syriac (and Armenian) translation. Very often the text had to endure tendentious revisions.[4] From these fragments it is necessary to piece together a coherent representation of the person and work of this most famous father of monks.

Unfortunately, we know very little about the youth and early career of Evagrius.[5] This little, however, may be viewed as certain, since Palladius undoubtedly came to know it from the mouth of his own teacher. Evagrius was born about 345 in Ibora (in present-day Turkey), in Pontus. His father was a chorepiscopus and, as one text assures us, "of aristocratic descent, one of the first in town." It has been assumed that Evagrius in his youth had been entrusted to Gregory of Nazianzus for training; however, nothing can be made of this with certainty. In his writings, in which he mentions Gregory several times, Evagrius himself does not refer to anything of the sort, as one would surely expect. Gregory himself seems to testify rather to the opposite.

However little we know about where Evagrius studied or to whom he had been apprenticed in his youth, it is apparent neverthe-

---

[4]For the literary work of Evagrius, see A. Guillaumont, *Évagre le Pontique: Un philosophe au désert* (Paris 2004), Second Part.

[5]For the Biography of Evagrius, see G. Bunge, *Briefe*, Introduction.

less from his later writings that he received an excellent all-round education. Above all, his knowledge of mathematics, philosophy, rhetoric,[6] and (naturally) theology may be praised. Such a comprehensive education was at that time even more expensive than today, and hence was accessible only to children of wealthy parents. Evagrius seems thus to have descended from a similar milieu as his later teachers and to have experienced a similar education.

At a date which unfortunately cannot be determined exactly, the young Evagrius was ordained a reader by Basil the Great (bishop from 370 to 379) and was admitted to the clergy of the Cappadocian metropolis of Caesarea. The claim that he had already been a monk in one of the monasteries reformed by Basil, rests on a misunderstanding: his *Letter 22* is addressed not to Basil but to Rufinus, and it refers to a much later time.

After Basil's death (January 1, 379) Evagrius makes his way, under circumstances which can unfortunately no longer be clarified, to the close friend of his deceased bishop, Gregory of Nazianzus, who was then bishop of Constantinople. There Gregory ordains him deacon and finds in the highly talented cleric a true friend and energetic supporter in his struggle against the Arians, still all-powerful in the imperial capital. Evagrius' earliest known writing, the *Epistula fidei* (*Letter on Faith*), composed in early 381, furnishes an eloquent testimony to this, just as Gregory's will, drawn up somewhat later, witnesses grateful affection. What role Evagrius played next to his bishop at the Second Ecumenical Council (381) has, unfortunately once more, not come down to us.

When Gregory, embittered by unending intrigues, withdrew from his position shortly thereafter (in the middle of 381), he left Evagrius to his successor Nektarios, who was still a layman at the time of his elevation. Nektarios learned to hold in high esteem the help of the deacon who by this time was more experienced in ecclesiastical and dogmatic questions.

But Evagrius' brilliant church career, of such great promise, came to an unexpected and abrupt end. The wife of a highly placed impe-

[6]See W. Lackner, "Zur profanen Bildung des Evagrios Pontikos," Fs. H. Gerstinger, Graz (1966), 17–29.

rial employee in the city became enamored of the brilliant orator, and in order to avoid a scandal Evagrius took to flight after receiving a vision in a dream. In 382 he left Constantinople secretly and made his way to Jerusalem, with the firm resolve to change his worldly life. He came to the decision to carry out his promise, however, only after a rare fever confined him to bed for half a year and brought him near death. At the request of Melania, a lady of high Roman nobility and an intimate friend of Rufinus, whose guest he was in Jerusalem, Evagrius received the monastic habit, certainly at Easter 383,[7] and immediately thereafter set out for the Egyptian desert, the classic land of monasticism. He lived there first for two years in the desert of Nitria, about 50 kilometers [31 mi.] southeast of Alexandria, and then, for the remaining years of his life, in the so-called "Kellia," located about 18 kilometers [11 mi.] deeper into the desert, where the monks led a more secluded, eremitical life. He died there at Epiphany 399.

*

Thus, like many monks at that time, Evagrius pursued a "late vocation," in no way entering the monastery in youthful zeal. Rather, it was the circumstances of life that had "banished him to the desert" almost against his will, a well-educated and spoiled Greek, as he himself once said.[8] This course naturally left its traces. Evagrius makes no secret of the fact that he did not find it easy to persevere all his life in the desolate desert. Nevertheless, he courageously resisted all temptations to return to the world, for example by not accepting the episcopal see of Thmuis offered to him by Theophilos, Patriarch of Alexandria.[9] In order to evade this honor, he fled to Palestine for a time, probably to his friends Rufinus and Melania.[10]

Evagrius' sacrifice was certainly not in vain. During the approximately fourteen years in the Kellia—doubtless less from a desire to speculate and more from obedience to a personal and strange existential need—his speculative mind developed a synthesis of practical

[7] *Ep* 22.
[8] *Ep* 50, 1.
[9] *Vita* G.
[10] *Vita* M.

and contemplative theology that would become classic. Numerous ascetical writings give eloquent testimony to his lifelong struggle. In these writings, destined mostly for anchorites and cenobites, Evagrius proves to be a thinker equipped with a rare sense of psychology and an analytical, penetrating insight. The numerous texts translated in this study provide us with a good overview of this aspect of his personality. Palladius, his student, presents a vivid image of the way of life of Abba Evagrius, who quickly achieved a certain celebrity, and of his work as a spiritual father.

> This was his habit: on Saturday and Sunday, the brethren gathered at his place; all during the night they discussed their thoughts with him, and listened to his words of encouragement until daybreak. Then they went away filled with joy and praised God, for Evagrius' teaching was very sweet.
>
> When they came to him, he addressed the following request to them: "My brethren, when one among you has a deep or troubled thought, let him be silent until the [other] brethren have withdrawn; then he may ask freely, when we two are alone. He should not reveal [his concern] to the brethren, so that a 'little one' may not be ruined or devoured by grief." Also, he was so hospitable that his cell took in no fewer than five or six strangers per day, who came to him from various places in order to become acquainted with his teaching, his intellect, and his ascetical practice. Indeed, he had at his disposal the money [needed for this], for many had sent him some. He had more than two hundred pieces of silver, which had been deposited with his administrator who always served in his dwelling place.[11]

This lively description of the life of Evagrius as spiritual father is confirmed in manifold ways from his own letters. In general, like all the anchorites of the Kellia,[12] during the entire week Evagrius lived in the seclusion of his cell (*kellion*). As archeological excavations in the Kellia have shown, his cell was rather a small house with several rooms and an enclosed yard, which, in addition to housing the spiritual

[11]*Vita* E. F.
[12]See A. Guillaumont, "Histoire des moines aux Kellia," *Aux origines du monachisme chrétien* (SO 30), Bellefontaine (1979), 151–167.

father, lodged his disciples and even accommodated guests who periodically visited from neighboring countries.[13] Here the father of monks devoted himself to prayer, contemplation, and manual labor; Evagrius was also a very talented calligrapher. On Saturdays and Sundays, the brethren, together with the guests who had arrived in the meantime, gathered for common prayer and then for conversation. Evagrius himself speaks very forcefully of the discretion which a spiritual father has to observe on such occasions.[14] Evagrius owes his unusual knowledge of the human soul to solitary introspection and to innumerable confessions of the heart.

From his disciple Palladius we learn further that Evagrius himself had an experienced monk, Albinus, who lived in his neighborhood, and in whom he confided in difficult situations.[15] Of course, nobody is his own spiritual father, not even the greatest desert abba.

This Albinus, like Melania and also Rufinus, was a noble Roman, and he appears repeatedly in the *Lausiac History* as belonging to the circle of Evagrius.[16] Since he was of Spanish descent, like Melania, and apparently also related to her, the supposition is warranted that the energetic Melania herself had entrusted her restless protégé to this elder. Evagrius held Albinus in high esteem, above all because of his exceptional meekness, a characteristic that he put above all other virtues since it singled out not only Moses[17] and David,[18] but especially Christ himself.[19] Above all, Evagrius counted meekness as the key to true knowledge of God.[20]

*

[13]See G. Descoeudres, *Kirchen und Oratorien in den Ermitagen der Mönchssiedlung Kellia*, Habilitationsschrift, Zürich (1994).
[14]See G. Bunge, *Geistliche Vaterschaft*.
[15]*Vita* 11 (at the End).
[16]See Bunge, *Briefe*, 32ff.
[17]Num 12.3.
[18]Ps 50.1 (LXX).
[19]Mt 11.29.
[20]*Ep* 56.

Based on his speculative writings, Evagrius has sometimes been called "the philosopher of the desert."[21] This characterization, which is found in the church historian Socrates, is correct if one interprets the concept of "philosopher" in the sense of Christian antiquity, as Socrates does. One understands "philosophy" in this sense preeminently as the perfect unity of Christian accomplishment in life and Christian knowledge of God. Evagrius himself speaks of Gregory of Nazianzus, "the mouth of Christ," as his "teacher in the highest philosophy."[22] In contrast, it would be misleading to consider Evagrius as a philosopher in the modern sense. He certainly had not persevered for sixteen years in the inhospitable Egyptian desert to devote himself to philosophical speculation. His goal as a *monk*, in whom Christian antiquity saw a "philosopher," a lover of divine wisdom, was purity of heart and the vision of God that flows from it. Philosophy in the technical sense of "dialectic" is, as Evagrius himself says, altogether superfluous.[23]

Evagrius' justly famous "psychology" has one aim only: to make the human being capable of loving again, and thereby capable of God. But this is not possible without overcoming the distortion of human existence and the passions that kill love. In turn, this overcoming is not possible without a specific knowledge of the working mechanisms of these passions and of their accomplices, the demons.

Evagrius is thus correctly to be described as a "master of the spiritual life" in the full and general sense of the term. Palladius, who knew him well, calls him "my teacher,"[24] the one who had introduced him into "the life in Christ" and had disclosed to him the meaning of a spiritual understanding of Holy Scripture.[25] In the *Sayings of the Fathers*, he is also accepted as "Abba" Evagrius, a learned monk, of course, but one who was above all a (spiritual) "father." It is essential to pay attention to this in his theological writings, if one does not want to misrepresent his image.

[21] See A. Guillaumont, "Un philosophe au désert: Évagre le Pontique," *Aux origines du monachisme chrétien* (SO 30), Bellefontaine (1979), 185–212.
[22] *Ep. fid.* 1, 14
[23] *Ep* 62, 1.
[24] HL 23; Butler, 75, 5.
[25] *Vita* Ab.

*

From the abundance of the spiritual teachings of Evagrius, we have singled out a special and, it seems to us, ever-present aspect: acedia (despondency). Others before and after Evagrius have spoken of acedia. In the *Apophthegmata, The Sayings of the Fathers,* it is mentioned in the first saying of Antony:

> When the holy Abba Antony lived in the desert he was beset by *accidie*, and attacked by many sinful thoughts. He said to God, "Lord, I want to be saved, but these thoughts do not leave me alone; what shall I do in my afflictions? How can I be saved?" A short while afterwards, when he got up to go out, Antony saw a man like himself sitting at his work, getting up from his work to pray, then sitting down and plaiting a rope, then getting up again to pray. It was an angel of the Lord sent to correct and reassure him. He heard the angel saying to him, "Do this and you will be saved." At these words, Antony was filled with joy and courage. He did this, and he was saved.[26]

This saying combines in itself an entire series of elements which we will find again in the spiritual teaching of Evagrius: the causes of despondency, its manifestations, and also the possible remedies.

Evagrius thus had at his disposal a definite tradition of the Fathers, which he made his own. Nevertheless, an actual "theory" of acedia is found first in him—and all writers after him have copied him more or less ably. Since for us it is not a matter of giving an exhaustive historical description of the phenomenon "acedia," but of exploring a specific spiritual teaching that can be of benefit to modern man, it seems permissible to restrict ourselves to the writings of Evagrius. We can do this all the more confidently, as Evagrius passes on not mere book knowledge, but his own experience. Thus, in one of his letters, he admits openly that this vice is not unknown to him:

> You have sought the one who "sits in darkness and in the shadow" of repentance, and you have "let a light beam forth" for the eyes that

---

[26]*Apophthegm Antonios* 1. [Trans. by Benedicta Ward, *The Desert Christian,* (MacMillan, 1975), 1–2].

unceasingly looked for consolation. What will I repay the Lord for the consolation of your letter, through which you have raised up my soul, which was tormented by acedia, and you remember "the dead dog": on account of the multitude of my depravities, I have been banished to the desert until today . . . [27]

Here, as so often in his personal letters, Evagrius does not present himself as a surpassing spiritual teacher, but he shows himself in all the vulnerability of his humanity. We will see also that his teaching stays closer to our human experience than one might at first assume.

From the abundant wealth of suitable texts, we have chosen and translated the ones that appeared to be most appropriate. Despite their occasional conciseness, these texts speak well for themselves and really need no commentary. Yet, since nearly all were originally composed for anchorites and cenobites, and thus for monks dwelling alone in the desert or living in a monastery, it seemed advisable to explain them a little and thereby make them more generally accessible. Let us therefore be forgiven for "having poured water into the wine."

[27]*Ep* 50, 1.

CHAPTER I

Acedia—A Disease Typical only of Monks?

M onasticism, still more its intense and original form, that of the anchorites, appears today to many (and not only to non-Christians) as a special existence, one established on the outskirts of "normal life," if it is not already beyond the border. For this reason, people readily talk about a "monastic spirituality"—even in monastic circles. The struggles and problems, the spiritual experiences and monastic methods, appear logically, even to believing Christians, as the special and particular domain of monasticism, without an organic connection to the life of "normal" Christians.

Many people will thus be tempted to put aside this little book immediately, since it deals indeed with the teachings of a father of monks. "What does he have to tell us today?" But if the reader has the courage to read to the end, then it may become clear to him that there exists here a fatal misconception. To be sure, this misconception has been widespread for a long time, and the monks themselves are not entirely blameless for its emergence.

If one believes the experts on the matter, then one of the most difficult problems the old monasticism, and chiefly the anchorites, had to deal with was *acedia*; and, for the time being, let this unfamiliar word stand. "Acedia, as defined by Evagrius, is essentially linked to the life of the anchorites and is typical of the one who chooses this state."[1] Is acedia therefore an exclusive disease of anchorites? For a judgment on this, A. Guillaumont can certainly appeal to such incon-

---

[1] A. Guillaumont, *Traité Pratique*, 89. The author has used this insight also in other studies on Evagrios.

testable authorities as John Cassian[2] and John Climacus.[3] Evagrius himself, in the treatise *De octo vitiosis cogitationibus* (*On the Eight Evil Thoughts*), which comes down to us under the name of Nilus of Ancyra, states laconically:

> The vice of acedia wages war above all on those who remain in seclusion.[4]

He seems to confirm this view when, in a letter to monks who had asked him for advice concerning the temptation to leave their house in case of acedia, he writes:

> To leave the physical house signifies a disgrace for [the monk], for it is the sign of defeat. But this happens to those who live for themselves alone.[5]

As he continues, however, Evagrius shows that he does not in the least think only of anchorites:

> For in Egypt, the monasteries were built by means of many [separate] cells, and each of the brethren makes his way alone for himself in his cell, working with his hands and praying. But they assemble in one place at the hour of refreshment and at the time of [common] prayer, scheduled in the morning and evening hours.[6]

This letter is addressed to monks who apparently lived as cenobites, though not in Egypt, perhaps in Palestine, who led a life that was apparently less isolated than the one Evagrius describes.

Likewise, two important statements on the theme of acedia, which we will encounter again, are found in two works, the so-called *Mirrors for Nuns* and *Mirror for Monks*, which unquestionably presuppose a cenobitic life, very likely the kind of life practiced in the

---

[2]Johannes Cassianus, *Conl.* X. 1. [In English, John Cassian, *The Conferences*, trans. by Boniface Ramsey. New York: Paulist Press (1997)].

[3]Johannes Klimakos, *Scala Paradisi*, gradus 13. [In English, *The Ladder of Divine Ascent*, trans. by Lazarus Moore. Boston (1976), and by Colm Luibheid and Norman Russell. New York: Paulist Press (1982)].

[4]PG 79: 1460A.

[5]*Ep* 27, 7 (in Greek).

[6]*Ep* 27, 7.

two monasteries on the Mount of Olives that Melania and Rufinus, friends of Evagrius, had founded in Jerusalem—therefore not desert monasteries but *urban.*

These observations, which will find much corroboration in the course of our account, lead us to a first important result: in the opinion of Evagrius, acedia is by no means an exclusive disease of anchorites! It overcomes those who live in community in exactly the same way. The contrary impression comes from the fact that Evagrius wrote mostly for anchorites, and thus for monks who, like himself, lived alone and occasionally came together with other brethren and visitors. Accordingly, his descriptions of acedia take into consideration the particular life circumstances of his readers.

*

Well and good, one may object, but what does that have to do with us? Indeed, we are neither anchorites nor cenobites but Christians who live in the midst of the world! The objection stems from the fatal misunderstanding mentioned at the beginning, that there is a particular world of monks and anchorites, whose problems basically do not affect "normal" Christians. An essential truth is thereby overlooked: the vices which plague humankind are the same from time immemorial and everywhere; only their concrete forms vary according to people's particular conditions of life. But acedia is one of the deadly vices! Evagrius himself states this very clearly:

> With men of the world, the demons fight mostly by means of things. However, with the monks, mostly through thoughts; for they lack things on account of their isolation.[7]

At another place, among "the monks," he differentiates still more precisely between anchorites and cenobites.

> The demons fight against the anchorites openly; against those who practice virtue in monasteries and communities, they arm the more negligent among their brethren.[8]

[7]*Pr* 48.
[8]*Pr* 5.

Therefore, Evagrius is of the opinion that the adversaries of human beings, that is, the passions or the demons that excite them, are the same the world over, although there are different levels in the intensity of the struggle. Lay people living in the world are tempted for the most part by concrete material things; those living together in a community and the cenobites, who live together in a narrow space, are tempted above all by their negligent brethren. There are all the small and large frictions of life in common, which indeed one is able to avoid far less in a monastery than in the world. The anchorites, on the other hand, who have given up not only material things, but largely also association with others, are tempted mostly by "thoughts," that is, by all the images, representations, and so forth that are inevitably left behind in their memories, not only of material things but also of inter-human connections and their problems.[9] These "thoughts" or memories represent the passions in their purest form, so to speak, detached from any direct concrete occasion. Evagrius declares pertinently that this struggle, "man against man," is by far the toughest, since no human being can be as malicious as a demon.[10]

This insight should make us think! Early monasticism was convinced of this: that in the desert the monk would meet no one else but "the prince of this world." Going into the desert with Christ does not mean to evade all temptations, but rather, with him, to learn how to confront the tempter "nakedly." It would be a disastrous illusion to think that this would be different today. The adversary of the human race is not tied to places, times, or conditions of life.

The one who enters a monastery today or devotes himself to the spiritual state does not consider, in our demythologized world, this fundamental reality: that he has *eo ipso* (by this very fact) entered the "desert," the place of isolation and abandonment, of desolate lean periods and misleading mirages. The one who does not want to acknowledge this, but believes he is only a brave "worker in the vineyard of the Lord," runs a great risk of failing to recognize the true nature of the difficulties he will certainly encounter. He will be surprised at the many "weeds," the "thorns and thistles," which his "vine-

[9]*M. c.* 25.
[10]*Pr* 5.

yard" bears instead of "grapes," and he will not understand that "an enemy" has sown these in cunning ways (Mt 13.24–30). These are not unforeseen episodes, but an integral component of life in the desert.

Paradoxically, one finds such an unsuspecting attitude not only among Christians living in the world, whose view is frequently obstructed by the opacity of material things, but even among monks and religious, who should know better. Acedia is an especially striking example, as we shall see. Where does such unawareness come from? Perhaps from this: that even monks and religious today no longer go deliberately with Christ into the open, merciless desert, but rather prefer to remain in the impenetrable world.

*

One may perhaps raise another objection: "Do not speak to us, you know, about the 'world' and the devil! These are old fables, which a person of our time no longer knows what to do with!"

It is true that it has become difficult to talk to modern man about evil as a "personal" power, so difficult that a contemporary biblical scholar has been able to advance the claim that one should, once and for all, make a clean sweep of "the myth of the devil." Meanwhile, the extent to which such an "enlightened" attitude ignores the reality of Scripture, a sound exegete like Heinrich Schlier in his study *Mächte und Gewalten im Neuen Testament* (*Principalities and Powers in the New Testament*) already demonstrated half a century ago.[11]

Could a poet perhaps have seen even more clearly than the biblical scholar? To cause fear of the devil, C. Baudelaire in his "Spleen of Paris" lets a "preacher, who was more discerning than his fellow brethren," make the following statement, which has become deservedly famous because of its cynicism and its clear-sightedness:

> My dear brethren, do not ever forget, when they praise the progress of the Enlightenment to you, that the most cunning trick of the devil is this: to convince you that he does not exist![12]

---

[11] *Quaestiones Disputatae* 3, Freiburg (1958). [In English, *Principalities and Powers in the New Testament*, Edinburgh: Nelson (1961)].

[12] *Oeuvres complètes* (Bibliothèque de la Pléiade), Paris (1951), 320.

Should we not hear this as frightful prophecy, the full significance of which even today we do not grasp? What will one say of this "bizarre affectation of boredom" that, according to the devil's opinion, "is the source of all our diseases and miserable progress?" But let us leave the poet of the *Flowers of Evil,* and let us return to the desert fathers, who have not lost any of their relevance.

*

In the texts here quoted, the discourse deals mostly indiscriminately with passions, thoughts, and demons. The thoughts are the carriers of the passions, and the demons are the authors of both. Without wishing to develop completely here the "demonology" of the desert fathers, or that of Evagrius in particular, the following observations are presented for consideration.

In a resolute stand against *Manichaean dualism* (as Evagrius probably experienced it in his immediate vicinity), the monk from Pontus looked upon evil as basically a pseudo-existence, a *privatio boni* ("deprivation of the good"). Evil's real character, however, is not thereby denied. What is resolutely rejected is only a metaphysical antithesis between two eternal principles.

Evagrius therefore objects with indignation to any slander against the Creator. Creation is good[13] and an expression of God's goodness[14] in its entirety and in all its parts. Above all, Evagrius turns emphatically against those who view the body as evil.[15] He puts a stop, in principle, not only to *suicide,*[16] but also to any asceticism that is hostile to the body, and any slow suicide through pious or impious motivations.[17]

As a pseudo-existence, evil has no continuous existence in itself, nor has the evil one. His wickedness is of a secondary nature, for "God has not created anything evil."[18] Even "the devil is not evil by

[13]Gen 1.
[14]*KG* III, 59.
[15]*KG* III, 53; IV, 60, 62.
[16]*KG* IV, 33, 76, 83.
[17]*Pr* 52.
[18]*KG* III, 59.

nature,"[19] but only on account of his misuse of freedom. Therefore, when we inveigh against the demons, for example, in order to keep them from our neck during prayer,[20] we do it not on account of their nature, but on account of their wickedness.[21] Evagrius draws the same distinction for sinful human beings. Man may be hateful on account of his ungodliness, as the psalm says; but as an image of God he is and always remains worth loving.[22] Consequently, there can be no justified anger against a fellow human being.[23]

Evil itself exists only as a parasite, in that it attaches itself as an alien entity to what was created good. From this insight, Evagrius draws the conclusion that the existence of evil is therefore not only secondary, but also finite.[24] "There was a time when evil did not exist, and the time will come when it will exist no more," for what is eternal is only what is in accord with the original creative will of God, the Good.[25]

But how does man experience evil (in the non-personal sense) and then the evil one as a personal power? As Evagrius' constant alternation between a "thought" (as a vehicle of the passions), a "passion," and a "demon" teaches, evil in the human domain can behave only as a parasite. So evil distorts the personhood of the man who perceives evil as personal in the "demon," insofar as he experiences himself as person. Outside the human realm, on the other hand, evil is experienced mostly as a nameless "principality" or "power," as it distorts the powers of creation.

As a rule, it is inordinately difficult, as we have said, for modern man to become aware of the personal character of evil, and thereby of the personal, evil power of Satan, and of the demons. That the satanic world is therefore all the more present in the fringes of society must, for all that, set one thinking. Could there not exist a secret link?

[19]*KG* IV, 59.
[20]*Pr* 42.
[21]*KG* V, 47.
[22]50 *in Ps* 118.113 (LXX).
[23]*Or* 24.
[24]See Wis 14.13.
[25]See *KG* I, 40. Cf. Wis 1.13–15.

The situation is altogether similar to that of the *sin-awareness* of
the Fathers, which has become entirely incomprehensible to modern
Western man. Against the awareness of being a sinner because one
has committed greater or lesser sins *in persona*, there is opposed today
a diffuse "feeling of guilt," from which not a few take refuge in aggressiveness against "society," when the pressure becomes intolerable.

A person is, of course, well aware that no one can free him from
this feeling of guilt, or perhaps guilt-complex, which is not due to
"sins" for which he is personally responsible. What is missing is what
is necessary for there to *be* sin: the personal Other, ultimately God,
against whom the human being has sinned. There is no forgiveness
for a generic "evil" or for "imperfections," because *only a person can for-
give another person.* Consequently, the experience of personal sinfulness—and also of forgiveness and the deliverance from all sins—is
linked to the experience of the Person of God.[26]

> The nearer a man draws to God, the more he sees himself a sinner.
> It was when Isaiah the prophet saw God that he declared himself
> "miserable, and a man of unclean lips."[27]

*

Much could be said about the deep background of a growing inability to perceive evil as a personal power—an inability which is praised
meanwhile by many enlightened souls as great "progress," even a true
"liberation." As has already been made clear, more is at stake than the
"devil." He can do very well without being perceived by human beings
as "really existing." Even more serious is the growing inability—
hardly noticed as such—to become aware of one's own personhood.
We are indeed witnessing a far-reaching process of depersonalization

---

[26]By this expression "Person of God," the author, as explained in correspondence,
intends to convey the experience of an *immediate relationship* between the *absolute
Person* of God and the *created person* of man, something only possible in Christ as
"the Image of God." The technical equivalent here is not *hypostasis*, but *prosōpon*, used
in the biblical sense of standing before God "face to face" (*prosōpon pros prosōpon;* see
1 Cor 13.12, cf. Ex 33.11).—*Ed.*

[27]*Apophthegm Matoes* 2 (Citation Is 6.5) [*The Desert Christian*, trans. by B. Ward
(1975), 143].

which ultimately threatens modern man himself in his very "being human."

What takes place before our eyes and in our hearts offers a partial view of an ultimately metaphysical event, which we are not able to see but can only "believe." Christianity—as a completion of the biblical revelation—is the *highest manifestation of the Person of God in the person of the human being.* In the person of the God-man Jesus Christ, the perfect self-revelation of the Person of God in his perfect incarnate "image,"[28] man first experiences himself as being created "in the image of God"[29] and consequently as a finite, created "person."

However, when this created "image" (*Abbild*) is severed from its uncreated "prototype" (*Urbild*), then one's experience both of the divine, and of human personhood, wanes at the same time. What remains is the "being delivered up" (*Ausgeliefert sein*), the "loneliness" of the modern human, "being thrown" (*Geworfenheit*). Admittedly, the saints were not spared this painful experience, but how differently it was lived by them! Let us remember the deeply perturbing answer Christ gave to Silouan the Athonite when he was confronted by the entire, concentrated personal power of the evil one: "Keep thy mind in Hell, and despair not!" This is an experience of the utmost remoteness of God, endured at the word of the Risen One, whose victory over death and the underworld we acknowledge in faith.

*

One may therefore make the paradoxical statement that one's consciousness of dealing with the evils in the world and with manifestations of personal evil powers in one's own soul, stands in a direct relation/proportion to one's consciousness of one's own personhood. Consequently, what is at stake is the human being's likeness to God, his fundamental reference to God, who in his triune being is the only Person in an absolute manner, and therefore alone brings about created personal being.

The downside of this general process of depersonalization is already obvious today. Where the awareness of the personhood of

[28]See 2 Cor 4.4; Col 1.15; Heb 1.3.
[29]Gen 1.27.

God, of one's own being, and also of the evil powers fades, there a diffuse and nameless anxiety streams in, one of being handed over to "evil" in an anonymous sense. This "evil" then manifests itself in history (politics, societal structures, and so on), in one's own life (impulse, heredity, environment, and so on), even in the cosmos (fate, the stars, and so on) in diverse ways, with man unable to escape from it. Rather, he finds himself delivered up to those "elements of the cosmos" from which the salvation of Christ has really freed him.[30]

One should not take lightly the causes that—not for the first time today, but today obviously and at the broadest level—have led to that loss of a center. Note the characteristic enthusiasm with which today's natural scientists, who are searching for a "new unity," turn to the non-personal religions of Asia or to forms of a never extinct Gnosticism. One may perhaps surmise that depersonalization is the last result (certainly not intended, and doubtless also not inevitable) of this scientific "Gnosis," which, in a particular moment of mankind's history, has become separated from the arts and from theology. With this separation (intended at first to be merely practical or tactical) was lost all reference to an absolute Other, the One who enables one's own self. Also lost was the very idea of unity, which is not "aloneness" but an unmixed oneness of the "I" in the sight of its "You."

But let us return to our desert fathers!

*

The keen feeling of our forefathers that they dealt with a personal evil power actually proves their high awareness of their own personal *gravitas*, their sense of their own freedom and responsibility for their own life. Evil thereby appears in its essence as an alien power that seeks to sneak up from the outside on their person, in order, once admitted, to warp them from the inside and thereby cause them to become estranged from God.

In the baptized person, who has sworn off Satan before witnesses, and who has died with Christ in the baptismal font and risen again, evil, in principle, has no more space to which it could lay claim. That

[30]Gal 4.

we, in spite of this, so frequently have the impression not only of being troubled, but of being practically dominated by evil, has its cause not, as the Messalians believed, in the demon inhabiting our heart even after baptism. No, the grace of baptism has driven him out completely, and light and darkness do not cohabit. Rather, it is on the grounds of heredity, the surrounding world, our own habits, our weakness of will, and so on, that the demon finds in us natural *allies*, as it were, of which he makes full use. It is an error to think, Evagrius says, that the demons know our heart. Only God, who created it, "knows the heart,"[31] but for the adversaries, it is indeed possible, through their allies, to transfer evil temptations into our heart—while we still remain free to accept or reject them.

All the striving of the Christian, and especially of the ascetic, is about eliminating these allies and refusing any "home rights" to the stranger. It is a question of cleansing the heart and keeping it clean. "Do not give the devil a foothold" (Eph 4.27).

The extraordinary living "demonology" of the desert fathers is basically nothing but a faithful mirror image of their extremely rich and sophisticated life of the soul. No wonder Evagrius lit upon that rich treasure of experience from which he developed his own strikingly sophisticated psychology. Far removed from the primitively unchristian anxiety about devils and witches that occurred in the Middle Ages, the demonology of the desert fathers is sustained by a fundamental optimism.

> But you should not think at all of that "fleeing serpent" (Is 27.1) that plagues you, and do not even consider him as anything, and do not be afraid of him. He is nothing but a runaway slave, who has lived badly and has escaped from his lord. Do not give him any foothold, until death! Our Lord has granted you to trample upon serpents and scorpions (Lk 10.19), and you are afraid of the voice of the demons while they howl? . . . The dragon knows only how to threaten.[32]

The stories of the monks are filled with priceless episodes in which the desert fathers ridicule the demons or simply rebuke them

[31]*M. c.* 37. See Apg I, 24; 15, 8.
[32]*Ep* 28, 2ff.

with perfect indifference. One of these stories, which Evagrius himself hands down to us, illustrates this trait of the old monastic spirituality.

> The demons approached another holy man living the solitary life in the desert. Since he prayed with great effort, they played ball with him for two weeks; they tossed him into the air and caught him on a small mat. But they absolutely did not succeed in drawing his intellect away even a little from his fiery prayer.[33]

In this case, complete disdain is indeed the only appropriate attitude toward the demons.[34]

*

This "personalizing" of evil, which seems grotesque to us, yet which a highly educated Greek like Evagrius did not scorn in the least, is by no means an expression merely of the more or less simple personality structure of a desert father. In the desert fathers is manifested an extremely alert and sober awareness of their own personal *gravitas* and responsibility. The struggle against the demons is basically a struggle for the integrity of their own person against any type of distortion through vice.

The struggle unfolds on different levels (though only on one level according to its nature): in the "world," where it is hardly recognized as such by the people, as it proceeds anonymously on the level of material things; in the life in common, where it rages in a secret way at the level of interpersonal relationships; and, in the absence of things and also of people, in the battle of the anchorites in the desert, where it is reduced to a struggle with "thoughts," the complex manifestations typical of spiritual life.

The third struggle is naturally by far the most difficult because man is completely thrown back upon himself, and no one is more to blame for his vice than he himself. Fundamentally, he struggles with himself for his own integrity, with his own unpurified heart from which evil thoughts well up, even without any provocation from out-

[33] *Or* III.
[34] *Or* 99.

side. Only vigilance and spiritual soberness protect him from being warped by evil.

*

The unusual external circumstances in which these professional fighters against the evil one have chosen to live sometimes cause the stories of the desert fathers to make a bizarre and exaggerated impression upon modern man, so much so that he incorrectly feels that they are irrelevant. Does not the same hold good for the desert fathers' evangelical "fundamentalism," which likewise delights us just as it bewilders us? Does not the following story, which Evagrius hands down to us, make sincere Christians feel deeply unsure?

> One of the brethren owned only a book of the Gospels, and when he had sold it, he gave [the proceeds] to feed the hungry as he made a remark that is worthy of remembrance: "I have sold the very word that tells me (Mt 19.21): 'Sell your possessions and give the proceeds to the poor.'"[35]

This is the concrete actualization of a thoroughly biblical principle that Evagrius formulated as follows in his *Praktikos*:

> It is impossible for charity to exist together in someone with possessions; for love is not only a destroyer of possessions, but even of this our transient life.[36]

Ultimately it is a matter of asking a fundamental question: is the Christian life, in its nature, its goals, its problems and methods, basically unified or not? In terms of the text quoted by Evagrius, the answer must be: there can be only *one* Christian vocation. Lay people and monks do not each have their own "spirituality," and the *Holy Spirit*, whom they all received in baptism, is one. The enemies and adversaries of the Christian are the same at all times no matter how well they disguise themselves. Victory will be gained also in one and the same manner, even when at first sight lay people and monks do not always put the same means into action.

[35] *Pr* 97.
[36] *Pr* 18.

But even here one should beware of illusions. Practices frequently categorized as "typically monastic," such as poverty, fasting, vigils, prayer, silence, and many others—all of them derive, without exception, from the writings of the New Testament and are therefore required of all Christians. The same holds true for life in the desert. For according to its nature, it is nothing else than the visible and highly symbolic expression of a separation from the "world," and its practices are demanded of each Christian. It is not, as one might suppose, that while one is in the desert, one is safe from the "prince of this world"! The case is rather the contrary, because the desert is the place where Christ first and fundamentally overcame evil, and because every Christian is called upon to engage himself in Christ's victory by his own personal decision.

In contrast to later generations, the first monks, who viewed themselves as imitators of the original Christian community and of the martyrs, had a very lively feeling for this, that ultimately they were nothing else but just Christians[37]—Christians indeed in a full and above all practical sense of the word, tending toward "fundamentalism." They knew they were in *the heart of the Church*, not on its outer periphery.

Therefore what happened to them had an exemplary meaning for the entire church, as did the life of the original Jerusalem community to which they had aligned themselves.[38] In a sense their life presents an extreme case, but is this not true for the early Jerusalem community as well? As frequently happens in such extreme situations, the essential witnesses step forward with unusual sharpness, and this is precisely what constitutes their exemplary value.

Whether monk or layman, cenobite or anchorite, the Christian has in the world, when he wants to imitate his Lord in loyalty, always one and the same experience, an experience ultimately none other than that of Christ himself. If one divests the extraordinary experiences of the anchorites and monks of their local and time-bound coloring, a core remains by which anyone can find his way back. If that were not so, people would hardly have taken the trouble to search out

---

[37]*M. c.* 6.
[38]See the example of Antony the Great, *VA* 2!

the desert fathers and seek their advice. Why would they have written down their "sayings" and passed them on from generation to generation?

The Christian East has never doubted this, and even today it still places monasticism at the center of its spiritual life. The apparently so visionary and "unworldly" experiences of the ancient desert fathers have a great deal to tell us. And not only their struggles but also their victories! The experience these desert fathers gained in their lonely life situations—the experience of human weakness, of being delivered to hostile powers from inside and outside, and also the experience of a concrete liberation from all these evils and of the grace-rich foretaste of heavenly magnificence—all this can indicate for the Christian living in the world today a path of liberation to authentic Christian being. It is enough to look carefully and listen attentively.

In times when the demons, formerly driven out by Christ, have returned under new names and in other disguises, more numerous than before, the commandment of the hour appears to be to name them once more by their correct names. This is all the more so because the quite incorrect opinion has spread that they should not be named at all. At such a moment, some believe that once and for all we have "demythologized" the *mysterium iniquitatis* (mystery of iniquity) and have finally transformed into pure imagination not only the evil one but also "so-called" evil. But then look! The one demon that is driven out returns with seven others that are worse, in order to seize the house all the more easily when they find it unguarded.[39]

In order to see clearly again it is necessary to dig up the "wells" our fathers dug previously in the desert by the sweat of their brow, which the "Philistines" in a malicious manner filled up again in the meantime. For it will not do that because of the lack of "living water" the people are obliged to make long trips—only to drink from the cloudy water of "Gihon,"[40] which the prophet has forbidden them

[39]Mt 12.43-45.

[40]In this allegorical-symbolic reading of the history of the patriarchs, which goes back to Origen, the "Philistines" signify pre-eminently "those of a different race" (*Fremdstämmigen*), the demons who prevent us from drinking at the well of "living water" of the knowledge of Christ. The "Gihon" is the Nile which flows in "Egypt," a symbol of the world and its wickedness on account of the sufferings of Israel in that place.

(see Jer 2.18). Once the old wells are dug up, and the water, cleansed
of desert sands, runs unhindered once more, then it will be seen that
even today it can quench the thirst of those who seek.

This conviction came to the author of these lines when, several
years ago, he read aloud a few pages from the manuscript of this little book to a group of young students who had asked him about his
work. Acedia was totally unknown to them. Yet when they heard a
few lines from the text of the monk of Pontus and I asked them,
"Does it tell you something?" they replied with a dismayed expression: "By all means, what your desert father describes is the evil of our
time." The next question then was raised: "And what can one do
against this?" Now, to that question, this little book will give an
answer.

CHAPTER 2

The Definition of Evil

A s we have said, acedia is first generally a "thought," one of the "eight generic thoughts,"[1] the classical listing of which goes back to Evagrius himself. In the linguistic usage of early monasticism, the concept of "thought" (*logismos*) is as ambivalent as the concept "world" in the New Testament, and indeed for the same reasons. In and of itself a thought is a natural and good manifestation of our soul-life, of our impressions and perceptions, our understanding of things in the world. In a subtle way, however, thoughts can become a vehicle for fixing one's aim not in accordance with creation. Then they gain the connotation of "evil thought," in the sense of an enticement to evil. As such they are revelations of the condition of our "heart," and they make visible its malice, its being uninterested in God, and its self-ruination.[2]

Thoughts understood in a positive as well as a negative sense have distinct origins. To those coming from the *senses*, the *memory*, and *temperament*,[3] are joined those which the *angels* and the *demons* prompt in us.[4] If the human being gives his consent to the latter—for everything depends on consent[5]—evil grows roots in us, and it becomes a "*habitus*" (habit) and then a passion (*pathos*) of the soul. The soul truly suffers then as from a disease, as Evagrius notes in one of his letters:

> However, concerning the passions that still dominate you, I think that the perception is this: of the thoughts that trouble us, some

[1]*Pr* 6.
[2]Mk 7.21.
[3]*Or* 62.
[4]*Ep* 18, 1; Pr 24:80.
[5]*Ep* 18, 5.

37

come indeed from nature, and others from the weakness of our will. Also from nature are those that happen to us from anger and desire. The ones that stem from nature trouble us through long duration, because the intellect imprints them on itself by thinking and is embraced by them, concerning which Scripture says: "Pass by quickly. Do not tarry at this place!"[6] However, those that come from the will bother the intellect when it assents to them. But it is written: "Do not desire to be with them."[7] Therefore, [thoughts] trouble us through lengthiness and the working of sin.

Natural thoughts are admittedly able to create even anger and desire [as well] in that they scatter the intellect through your many occupations; let it [your intellect] then make every endeavor to take appropriate remedies, namely hunger, thirst, vigils, withdrawal from the inhabited world, and prayer . . . .[8]

At first glance this passage could create the impression that Evagrius considers thoughts to be what we call a "hereditary disease." Meanwhile, with "nature," "blood," and "the parents," something entirely different is meant, as we learn from the rest of the letter, and related texts. Let us remember that for Evagrius no evil can come from *nature*, since this indeed means the original reality of creation. A "thought which comes from human nature" is, for example, one "by which, even the pagans, when moved by it, love their children and honor their parents."[9] Also, what is meant are those "seeds of virtue," the indestructibility of which Evagrius is convinced, which are therefore common to all human beings, even the worst sinners.[10]

Nevertheless the demons are able to make use of "thoughts" that are good in themselves, for example when they distort the natural love of parents and children, and play it off against the love of God. Evagrius observes that Christ speaks of this, that no one can follow him if he does not "hate"[11] father, mother, brother, and so on. Evagrius

[6]Prov 9.18.
[7]Prov 24.1.
[8]*Ep* 55, 2ff.
[9]*Ep* 18, 1.
[10]*KG* I, 40.
[11]*Ep* 55, 3.

observes accurately that these thoughts are extraordinarily long-lived since the ties of blood are indeed the strongest. But Evagrius is no fatalist. The human being is delivered neither to these natural thoughts, nor to those that stem from his weakness of will, any more than he is to demonic promptings.

> Three thoughts are opposed to demonic thought, and they cut it off, if it persists in our thinking. The first is the one from the holy angels that stirs in us in a hidden way. The second is the one that stems from our own will's leaning toward what is proper to it. The third is the one which stems from human nature, at whose prompting even the heathen love their children and honor their parents.[12]

Our "thoughts" are very *complex structures*. It is fundamental that for Evagrius "nature" is good;[13] however, this good can be warped in various ways. The demons are able to distort not only our natural feelings, but even our memory, just as they can influence our physical condition.[14]

*

Meanwhile, free will stands opposed to all such machinations in that it *decides* whether we incline toward good or evil. The greatest difference between classical and modern psychology probably lies in the former's heavy emphasis on free will. Like all classical antiquity, Evagrius does not know the modern concept of a "child," which for him counts only as a little adult. He therefore does not know, either, the problem of heredity or of early childhood formation. For this reason, his portrait of the human being appears as a free and responsible being with a wholly natural, that is, indestructibly created, goodness, which is a person's existential reference to God. The entire goal of the demons is to warp and distort this goodness.

> With what purpose do the demons excite in us gluttony, impurity, greed, anger, rancor, and the other passions? [They want] our intel-

---

[12]*Ep* 18, 1.
[13]*Ep* 18, 2.
[14]*Or* 69.

lect, coarsened through these [passions],[15] not to be able to pray as it ought. For the passions of the irrational part [of the soul], once they have acquired sovereign power, do not allow the intellect to function properly and search for God the Word.[16]

The ultimate aim of all asceticism, which is perfect *passionlessness*, consists therefore of this: to rule "rationally" over the irrational powers of the soul[17] and finally to leave behind also the dispassionate, "simple" thoughts[18] in order to go "immaterially to the Immaterial."[19]

> *Let my prayer arise in thy sight as incense.* Like incense does the prayer arise of the one who can say: "For we are to God the sweet smell of Christ among those who are being saved and those who are perishing."[20] And there is one form of prayer which leaves the intellect without impress: the conversation of the intellect with God. I call an intellect "unimpressed" which, at the time of prayer, does not imagine anything material. For only those names and words that signify something sensual imprint and mold our intellect. In prayer, the intellect must therefore be free of everything sensual. But the thought of God leaves the mind of necessity without imprint, since [God] is not a body.[21]

*

The eight "thoughts," understood in a pejorative sense, always appear in a fixed order, which only occasionally undergoes a rearrangement at one position: gluttony, lust, avarice, sadness, anger, acedia, vainglory, and pride.[22] Evagrius names these eight thoughts "generic," because not only are all other thoughts generated from them, but these eight themselves are interwoven in many various ways. Either one proceeds from another, or they stand in superficial opposition to

[15]What is meant is that the intellect succumbs to the weight of the body.
[16]*Or* 51.
[17]*Gn* 2.
[18]*Or* 56–58.
[19]*Or* 6.
[20]2 Cor 2.15.
[21]I *in Ps* 140.2.
[22]*Pr* 6.

one another.[23] To be sure, acedia occupies a special place as we shall see.

Occasionally Evagrius reduces these eight thoughts into three: gluttony, avarice, and vainglory, which form the frontline, as it were, behind which stand the battalions of the other thoughts.[24] Here the temptations of Christ in the desert serve as a model; as a rule, these occupy Evagrius' attention to a high degree.[25] Whether there are only three or eight generic thoughts, they have their common root in "love of self" (*philautia*), which in itself remains outside the list.[26] As a rule Evagrius does not return to this fundamental root, but we have to keep it before our eyes in order to be able to understand the mechanism of the thoughts and the role acedia plays in this evil concert.

Eight *virtues* stand opposed to the eight thoughts: temperance, prudence, poverty, joy, forbearance, patience, moderation, and meekness.[27] Self-love, for its part, has its counterpart in love, which as a basic attitude also remains outside the list.

*

The eight virtues, along with the eight generic "thoughts," are common to all human beings—the virtues, certainly, as they belong to our created nature;[28] the "thoughts" in so far as the demons contend against everyone, though against each person in a different manner. The eight "thoughts" are by no means to be viewed as sins as long as it is a matter of tempting persuasions, and no one should feel ashamed of them.

> Whether or not all these thoughts disturb the soul does not depend upon us. However, whether they linger or do not linger, arouse our passions or not, that depends on us.[29]

---

[23] *Pr* 45.
[24] *M.c.* 1.
[25] *Ant Prol; Ep* 6, 2–3; 39, 3.
[26] *Sk* 53.
[27] *Vit.*
[28] *KG* I, 39.
[29] *Pr* 6.

What turns these "thoughts" into passions and then into *sins* is the *voluntary consent* of the human being, who gives way to evil within himself.

> Temptation in a monk is a thought that arises through the passionate part of the soul (that is, anger and desire) and darkens the intellect.[30]

> A sin for a monk is the [free] consent [of the will] to the forbidden pleasure of the thought.[31]

The mechanism which triggers the passions in individual cases is not easy to see through. Do the ideas which are impressed upon our mind cause the passions, or is it the other way around?[32] Since every desire arises from a *sensory impression*[33] and "all demonic thoughts introduce into the soul images of sensory objects,"[34] Evagrius decides on the first-named solution, that sensory impressions normally trigger the passions in us,[35] provided that we consent to them. In order to prevent consent we need the virtues, and, to be precise, above all we need these two, which keep a tight rein on the passionate part of the soul: love as a bridle for anger, and self-control as a rein on desire.[36] If both of these rule in the soul, the sensory impressions will not trigger the passions.[37]

In a certain sense, therefore, the passions have their origin in us, namely in the lustful mode in which we take up the impressions that material things evoke in us.[38] Going further, we can distinguish between passions of the *soul*, which derive from inter-human relationships, and those of the *body*, which emerge from its needs.[39] The latter are comparatively easy to control by means of asceticism. The

[30] *Pr* 74
[31] *Pr* 75.
[32] *Pr* 37.
[33] *Pr* 4.
[34] *M.c.* 2.
[35] *Pr* 38.
[36] *Pr* 35.
[37] *Pr* 38.
[38] *Pr* 34.
[39] *Pr* 35.

former, on the contrary, pursue a human being until death,[40] for instance, anger.[41] Even the most severe asceticism is not able to change this. Evagrius perceptively observes that anger, a passion of the soul, plagues above all the old, while the young have to deal with the stomach, a bodily passion.[42] Progress in the spiritual life does not consist in what is understood today as "apathy"!

> A burning arrow[43] inflames the soul, but a man who practices virtue puts it out. [44]

> The virtues do not hinder the assaults of the demons, but they keep us unharmed.[45]

*

Tracing the passions back to their origin in man's consent signifies how for Evagrius evil does not lie in human nature. Such an assertion would slander the Creator.

> When we were created in the beginning, we had in us the seeds of virtue, not those of evil. For if we become susceptible to something, then do we not also possess the implicit capacity for it? . . . [46]

Evil has its origin rather in the misuse we make of our good gifts:

> All malice is generated by understanding, anger, and desire; it is, however, possible to make good or bad use of these powers. Thus it is obvious that evil happens to us through our perverse use of this part [of the soul]. Therefore, if that is so, there is nothing created by God that is evil [by nature].[47]

By "perverse use" Evagrius understands, like most theologians of the Eastern Church, a use that runs contrary to the Creator's purpose.

[40]*Pr* 36.
[41]*Pr* 38.
[42]*Gn* 31.
[43]See Eph 6.16. The reference is to a symbol of demonic thought.
[44]*Mn* 70.
[45]*Pr* 77.
[46]*KG* I, 39.
[47]*KG* III, 59.

Nature is and remains good, and a good that cannot be lost. Sin and the passions are always only alien bodies, which can and will be excluded. To the extent that evil is not eternal[48] it exists merely as a parasite, and it will disappear along with whatever has provoked it. Evagrius finds a confirmation of this in the Gospel itself:

> There was a time when evil did not exist, and the time will come when it will exist no more. However, there was never a time when virtue did not exist and there will be no time when it will no longer be. For the seeds of virtue are imperishable. The rich man convinces me of this; he was in hell because of his malice yet took pity on his brothers. But having compassion is an excellent seed of virtue.[49]

This conviction of the imperishable goodness of creation and of the essential nothingness of evil gives the whole of Evagrius' asceticism its typical, optimistic vigor—without doing the slightest damage to its seriousness.

*

A western reader marked by the theology of Augustine may well sense a veiled *Pelagianism* in this optimism. Indeed, Jerome attempted, wrongly, to enroll the monk from Pontus among the foster-fathers of Pelagius because of his teaching on *apatheia* (passionlessness). Evagrius is far removed from denying God's grace or disparaging it. Nothing was further from him than arrogant self-realization. He advises especially the "perfect one," tempted by arrogance, to recall to whom he owes his dispassion: to the mercy of Christ!

> Think also about this: who protects you in the desert? Who removes the demons that grind their teeth against you?[50]

These, and similar reflections,[51] are suitable for leading a human being back to the solid ground of facts and making him humble. The

---

[48]*Ep* 43 *et frequenter.*
[49]*KG* I, 40.
[50]*Pr* 33.
[51]See *O. sp.* 8, II.
[52]12 *in Ps* 17.21.

secret of the spiritual life consists neither in a one-sided *sola gratia* (grace alone) nor in the lone and self-empowered effort of the human being, but rather in *synergia*, the working-together of "divine grace and human zeal,"[52] whereby it is beyond question that the Creator has not only the first but also the last word.

> It depends on us to achieve virtue with the power of God; on the contrary, it does not depend on us to be made worthy of spiritual knowledge.[53]

The entire spiritual life, both its "practical" asceticism as well as in a narrower sense its "contemplative," mystical life is a mysterious teamwork between the infinite Person of the triune God and the created person of the human being. Thanks to a growing "*harmony of wills*"[54] between the Creator and creation, the Creator takes an ever stronger lead, until life becomes truly "spiritual," that is, permeated entirely by the working of the Holy Spirit.

Accordingly, Evagrius never tires of emphasizing that the goal of our spiritual striving, the contemplation or knowledge of God, can only be *bestowed* on the human being: he is "deemed worthy of it," as Evagrius says pointedly in numerous places. The "Gnostikos," the [contemplative] counterpart to the "Praktikos," is therefore destined for the one "who has been deemed worthy of knowledge" (the subtitle of the "Gnostikos").

*

The time has finally come to define *acedia* more accurately. Like so many concepts of the ascetic-technical monastic vocabulary, *acedia* is overloaded with so many and various shades of meaning that it is nearly impossible to express it adequately with a single word. Long ago John Cassian already faced the dilemma: "*Sextum nobis certamen est quod Graeci* akēdian *vocant, quam nos taedium sive anxietatem cordis possumus nuncupare*": "Our sixth combat is with what the Greeks call *acedia*, which we may term tedium or anxiety of the heart."[55]

[53]3 *in Ps* 43.4.
[54]*Ep. Mel.* 23, 26.
[55]*Inst* X, 1. [English trans. in *The Twelve Books of John Cassian on the Institutes of*

Despite this excellent attempt at translation, Cassian is subsequently satisfied most of the time with a mere transliteration: *acedia*. Of all possible English equivalents—*repulsion, boredom, inertia, indolence, lassitude, dislike, dejection, despondency*—the last seems to us to be the most appropriate, if it is understood that in the term *despondency* the other shades of meaning are heard together. Meanwhile, we will keep it frequently as Cassian does and speak simply of *acedia*.

Now, precisely what does Evagrius understand by *despondency*? One definition will lead us forward:

> "*You will not be afraid . . . of the assault of the noonday demon*":
> The noonday demon, it is said, is the demon of *acedia*.[56]

When he resumes at another place, Evagrius appeals to a tradition (known also to Cassian)[57] that he could have found in the *Commentary on Psalms* by Athanasius:

> The demon of despondency, also called "the noonday demon," is the most oppressive of all demons. He attacks the monk at the fourth hour and encircles the soul until the eighth hour.[58]

Anyone who has ever resided in the east will recall the context of this image. The time between the fourth hour (10:00 a.m.) and the eighth hour (2:00 p.m.) is, at it were, the "dead point" of the day. The sun is at its highest; the heat is unbearably oppressive, and it causes all the powers of life and of the soul to fall asleep. The human being loses all desire to do anything. Usually during this time all the shops are closed, and life stands still for a few hours. During this time the "noonday demon" has a special taste for moving around, especially among the monks, since they, unlike other people, were not in the habit of lying down even a little. Only the evening brings relief, when monks traditionally take their first and only meal of the day after the ninth hour (3:00 p.m.).

---

the Coenobia, in *NPNF* (Nicene and Post-Nicene Fathers), second series, vol XI, rept. 1978, 266].

[56] 4 *in Ps* 90.6.
[57] *Inst* X, 1.
[58] *Pr* 12.

Acedia manifests itself, then, as a type of slackening of the natural powers of the soul. Evagrius defines it in exactly the same way:

> Spiritual despondency is a slackness (*atonia*) of the soul, namely a limpness of the soul, which does not possess what is appropriate to its nature.[59]

It would, of course, be an error to think that this "growing slack of the soul's tension (*tonos*)"[60] is linked to a certain time of the day; in other words, that the "noonday demon" makes his rounds only at the time of noon. By contrast, he is no less active during the night!

> At the time of the *synaxis* (gathering),[61] when the spirit of despondency attacks you, he suggests to your soul that psalmody is wearisome, and with the greatest zeal he hurls reluctance as an opponent to zeal, so that the soul in a great hurry hands the flesh over to the memory that it is exhausted for some reason or other.
>
> When we keep vigil at night, therefore, let us not surrender the synaxis to despondency, lest the demons who stand around collect the weeds of thought and sow them at once in the heart.[62] For when we destroy the collection of hymns, then we gather together the collection of thoughts.[63]

*

A slackening of the tension of the soul, a feeling of emptiness and listlessness, moroseness, the inability to concentrate on a single task, lassitude and weariness of heart (Cassian)—who would claim that this state of soul (*état d'âme*) is proper only to anchorites? The ancient philosophers knew it well, and the church fathers speak of it. In the modern age this "perhaps most painful human phenomenon" (Romano Guardini) seems to have acquired even more depth and power. Pascal's *ennui* (boredom) and Kierkegaard's *melancholy* com-

[59] *O. sp.* 6, 1.
[60] *O. sp.* 6, 16.
[61] What is meant is the monastic Office.
[62] See Mt 13.25.
[63] *Eul* 9.

pellingly grip one; and what will one say about *Angst* (anxiety), the twin sister of acedia as we shall see? Has it not become the mark of Cain on our civilization?

It would be very instructive to compare the thoughts of Evagrius with those of modern thinkers who are not influenced by monastic literature. Let it be left to the reader to do this himself.[64] For us, let it suffice to continue investigating the insight of our most influential desert father.

*

One cannot close one's mind to the insight that acedia is not at all a disease only of anchorites. If this were so, then the anchorites would have done better to leave their desert solitude as quickly as possible! Rather, despondency—like a shadow—is linked indissolubly with our human condition. Yet in no way do we exclude that it can assume very different forms.

As we shall see, acedia is the religious-metaphysical dimension, so to speak, of a common human "suffering," which in its secular form is experienced as *ennui* (boredom), melancholy, depression, and so forth. While the human being—subjectively—suffers above all from himself, and from others like himself, acedia also, as Evagrius says, "darkens" one's relationship to God. Whether one admits it or not, the reference to God is inherent in every human being.

Finally, between worldly people (*kosmikoi*) and monks (*monachoi*) there exists a slight distinction, at most, insofar as the latter live out their humanity consciously in its deepest metaphysical dimension. The "man of the world" thinks from the perspective of "the world"— the monk, from God's point of view. In this sense, Evagrius defines "monk" not in a typical "monastic" fashion as "monastic brother"; neither is his "anchorite" merely a "desert father."

The true monk is distinguished by this: that he is *"separated from all, and united harmoniously to all."*[65] *"He regards himself as linked with*

---

[64]See the minor text by R. Guardini, *Vom Sinn der Schwermut* (Mainz, 1983), and the important biographical background study by H-B. Gerl, *Romano Guardini 1885–1968*, (Mainz, 1985), with the Excursus, "Die Schwermut," *op. cit.* 310–316.

[65]*Or* 124.

every man by always seeing himself in each."[66] Such a monk, then, is in no way merely a solitary man; rather, he is perfectly *united to all*! Similarly, the anchorite has not only withdrawn (*anachōrēsis*) from the inhabited land, but "*lives piously and uprightly in the world that exists in the mind.*"[67]

In the end, the program of the monk of Pontus is the business of everyone regardless of where he lives; it is certainly a program with wide horizons. Not only should the "man," but also the inmost and essential part of this "man"—his "intellect"—become a "monk" (i.e. be freed from all sinful acts).

> A monk-intellect is the one who turns away from the sin that arises from the thoughts that are in our soul, and who, at the time of prayer, contemplates the light of the Holy Trinity.[68]

As it turns out, acedia is the largest stumbling block on the road to this wonderful enlightenment. It is therefore worthwhile to study this arch-evil in detail, if one does not want to incur the loss of the deepest experience a human being can have in this life.

---

[66] *Or* 125. [*The Philokalia. The Complete Text.* Vol I, trans. by G.E.H. Palmer, Philip Sherrard, and Kallistos Ware. (London: Faber & Faber, 1979), 69].
[67] *Sk* 14.
[68] *Ant Prol* 7.

CHAPTER 3

The Origin and Characteristics of Vice

In order to treat an illness successfully, one should be in a position to determine accurately its origin and nature. This remains true also for the passions (*pathē*) of the soul. Evagrius therefore ascribes great significance to the exact diagnosis of processes within the soul:

> One must also recognize the differences between the demons and note their temporal circumstances. Now, we will recognize from the thoughts (and on the basis of the thoughts, from [material] things) which demons appear more seldom and with greater force, and, respectively, which ones appear constantly and with lesser force, as well as which demons burst in all of a sudden and entice the mind to blasphemy. It is necessary to know this, so that when thoughts begin to suggest their proper material but before we have been utterly cast out from our own state—we may bring something against them and make the present demon known. In this way, we will easily make progress with God's help; but we shall force those demons, distressed and full of wonder at us, to take flight.[1]

The text in fact indicates what kind of associations these are. The thoughts arise from contact with material things, or rather the sensory impressions they evoke.[2] In order for "thoughts" in the pejorative sense to result from these thoughts or impressions, they must be received in a manner marked by passion,[3] that is, be distorted in a selfish way.

[1]*Pr* 43.
[2]*Pr* 38.
[3]*Pr* 34.

According to their nature, all passions have a dual origin, corresponding to the dual nature of the human being, body and soul.[4] In so far as the intellect is the "head" of the soul,[5] it is also affected by these passions, for example by the blasphemy of which we spoke earlier. "Blasphemy" is a typical expression of the vice of arrogance,[6] which, in turn, is a product of vanity,[7] which imagines itself as being wonderful, having subdued the other demons by its own power. This spirit of blasphemy drags the intellect into blasphemy.

From this example, one recognizes the subtle ways in which thoughts are "interwoven"[8] with one another. It becomes clear in which sequence the eight generic thoughts stand: the coarse and sensual come in front, followed by their immediate successors; at the end stand the more immaterial, those that prepare for the higher rungs of spiritual life when the other passions have been overcome. Vanity and pride are the typical vices of the "perfect."[9]

Despondency comes in about the middle, as it is both the endpoint of the baser and the beginning of the more subtle passions. Yet vanity and arrogance always end up among the lowest passions. Thus, vanity with pride or sadness often ends with impurity;[10] pride, for its part, ends with anger or sadness, if not with complete mental confusion.[11] And from anger or sadness, despondency develops again, as we shall see.

It is therefore absolutely necessary to understand precisely the subtle mechanisms of the thoughts, if one does not want to be led by the nose around one's own desires. Ultimately, this can be done only by way of careful *self-awareness* joined to prayer for insight.[12] How difficult this is Evagrius acknowledges in a letter.[13] Since it is largely

---

[4]*Pr* 35.
[5]*KG* V, 45.
[6]*Ant* VIII, 41.
[7]*Pr* 13.
[8]*Pr* 50.
[9]*Pr* 13.
[10]*Pr* 13.
[11]*Pr* 14.
[12]*Pr* 50.
[13]*Ep* 4, 1.

a question of empirical knowledge, not a prefabricated traditional system, one may not expect from Evagrius a strong logical coherence. His psychological writings were set down over the course of more than fourteen years, and it is to be accepted *a priori* that in the course of time his insight into the intertwining paths of the life of the soul deepened more and more. Since he himself has not given a comprehensive account of his psychology, it is neither possible nor meaningful to distil such a closed system from his work. On the whole, where acedia is concerned, however, his basic intuitions do not seem to have changed.

*

Despondency is certainly one of the eight generic "thoughts," but it is very different in nature from the rest. If it is true that, for the others, at any given time they are a link in a colorful and variously assembled chain, so it is said of despondency that it is always the *terminus* of such a chain, and is therefore not followed immediately by any other "thoughts."

For obvious reasons, an especially close relationship exists between despondency and sadness, and indeed in the sense that sadness develops into despondency. Thus, for instance, one can fall into despondency from sadness over the all-powerful temptation of impurity.[14] Evagrius names both thoughts very frequently in one breath.[15] He says:

> Despondency:
> partner of sadness.[16]

Or the reverse:

> Sadness:
> schoolmate of despondency.[17]

---

[14]*Ant* II, 12.
[15]*Ant* II, 64; IV, 35, 37; VI, 31, 49 *et passim.*
[16]*Vit* 4.
[17]*Vit* 3.

Sadness and despondency are therefore not identical; but they are nonetheless so closely related to one another that what Evagrius says about the former applies to a large extent to the latter. Hence, in what follows, we will occasionally use texts about sadness in order to understand better the phenomenon of despondency. In the meantime, we must refrain from portraying sadness in detail; the texts are so numerous they would fill a book of their own.

*

The characteristic difference between sadness and despondency becomes clear in the following texts. Evagrius defines the origin of sadness as follows:

> Sadness arises out of a failure of a fleshly desire, and a desire is linked to each passion.[18]

Therefore at the root of acedia lies the frustration of a desire. But for despondency to arise from sadness, something else must still be added:

> Acedia is a simultaneous, long-lasting movement of anger and desire, whereby the former is angry with what is at hand, while the latter yearns for what is not present.[19]

Evagrius expresses the same thought in a text that at first sight is downright peculiar:

> Of thoughts, some occur to us as animals; others, however, as human beings. The ones [occurring to us] as animals are those that come from desire and anger; but [the ones occurring to us] as human beings are those that come from grief, vainglory and arrogance. On the other hand, [thoughts] that come from despondency strike us as animals as well as human beings, since they are mixed.[20]

To what extent can one call a human being an "animal"? For this is how the "*zōon*," generally signifying "a living being," is to be translated. The following texts teach us what is meant:

---

[18] *O. sp.* 5, 10.
[19] See 13 *in Ps* 118.28.
[20] *Sk* 40.

Sometimes the demons confuse a man insofar as he is a rational being [*logikon*], and sometimes insofar as he is an irrational being [*alogon*]. In particular, if the attack occurs with respect to the irrational [a-logical] part of the soul—I mean to say anger and desire—then [the demons] move this part in the manner of irrational beings. With respect to these [two irrational parts] this movement also occurs with irrational animals.[21]

Indeed, a human being has both a-logical, irrational powers of the soul, the *thymikon* (incensive power) and *epithymētikon* (desiring power) in common with the animals, together with his body.[22] As long as he moves on the level of these two powers, according to Evagrius, he is not essentially different from an animal. He is simply a "living being" (*zōon*). That is why, in his *Letter to Melania*, Evagrius puts together a long list of all those emotions that we have in common with the animals.[23] Modern behavioral researchers may wonder which feelings, as a rule operative as "typically human," can be recognized also in the animals, or, to put it better, to what extent does a human being react like an animal? For it is a matter of irrational stirrings that belong entirely to the domain of instinct.

A second text develops further the distinction between "human" and "animal" passions. It clearly teaches in what, for Evagrius, the *specifically human* consists: not in the feelings, no matter how sublime they may appear to us, but in everything that belongs to the "intelligent" (*logistikon*) power. The human being is a human being in so far as he is *logikon*, a being gifted with *logos* (reason). His likeness to God is based on his participation in the *divine logos*, his ability to know God, which is the most important expression of his being a person, whose imperishable treasure is the "intellect" (*nous*).

This has nothing to do with "intellectualism."[24] The German concept "*erkennen*" (to perceive, discern) is ambiguous. It is a purely

[21]J. Muyldermans, *À travers la tradition manuscrite d'Évagre le Pontique*, Bibliothèque du MUSÉON 3, Louvain (1932), 90, f. Nr. 44.

[22]*KG* VI, 85.

[23]*Ep. Mel.* 41.

[24]See G. Bunge, "Nach dem Intellect leben." Zum sog. "Intellektualismus" der Evagrianischen Spiritualität, *Simandron der Wachklopfer*: Gedenkschrift für Klaus Gamber, ed. by W. Nyssen, Cologne (1989), 95–109.

external contemplation of this world, that of the "ways of this world."[25] That contemplation is "coarse" and accessible also to demons, the godless, and the impure[26]; its preferred technical means is "dialectic."[27] It cannot impart more than the outer aspect of reality.[28] Contrasted to it is "spiritual knowledge" which alone can grasp the nature of things, and which is accessible only to the pure, "the contemplatives";[29] that is, only to the "pure intellect," for only this is *capax Dei*, capable of receiving God.[30] Here now is our text:

> Of the unclean demons, some tempt the human being as a human being, while others confound man as an unreasoning animal. Now, when they come near, the first whisper to us thoughts of vainglory or arrogance or envy, or the mania to criticize—things that do not affect any of the beings devoid of reason. On the other hand, when the second draw near, they arouse an unnatural anger and desire, those passions which we have in common with the irrational animals, but which are concealed in us beneath rational nature. For this reason, the Holy Spirit says to those with the property of human thought: "*I have said: 'you are gods, and all of you children of the Most High.' But you will die as men and fall as one of the princes.*"[31] And what does he say to those who are stimulated in an animal (alogical) manner? "*Be ye not as the horse and mule, which have no understanding; whose jaws thou must hold with bit and bridle, lest they come nigh unto thee.*"[32]

Finally, a third text clarifies what Evagrius understands by a "blending" of thoughts of despondency.

> All day long they provoke war.[33] The demons fight against us through thoughts, in that from time to time they stimulate desire,

[25]*KG* I, 73; VI, 22.
[26]*KG* VI, 2.
[27]*KG* IV, 90.
[28]*KG* I, 32.
[29]*KG* I, 32; IV, 90.
[30]*KG* III, 24; see II, 3.
[31]Ps 81.6–7.
[32] *M.c.* 18. The last quotation, Ps 31.9.
[33]Ps 139.3.

from time to time anger; and then at the same time anger and desire, as a result of which emerges the so-called complex thought. This occurs at the time of despondency, while the others, taking turns, follow at a distance. But on this day, no other thought follows that of despondency, first because it persists, and then also, because it contains in itself nearly all the thoughts.[34]

*

With that, the most important elements are given. All passions arise from the *passionate part* of the soul, that is, from desire and anger, by which we communicate with the world of the senses,[35] and which we have in common with the unreasoning animals. From there they ascend and darken the mind,[36] that is, they hinder it in its most characteristic work—attaining knowledge.[37]

Now, while the other passions emerge from one of the two irrational powers of the soul, despondency is marked by this: that it consists of a "blending" or an "interweaving" of thoughts from both.

Settled entirely in the a-logical domain, acedia is therefore a phenomenon that is *irrational* to the highest degree! For that reason, with evident pleasure, Evagrius in one of his letters describes the poor "animal" plagued by acedia in the following words:

Concerning the thought of despondency, you have written to me: which house does it compel us to leave, perhaps the intelligible or the sensory? Which does the one tempted by this temptation hate above all things? Alone among the thoughts this one is an "interwoven" one, since it results from hatred and desire. A despondent person hates precisely what is available, and desires what is not available. To the extent desire pulls down the monk, so also does hatred chase him from his cell. He is to be viewed as an unreasoning animal, dragged by desire and beaten by hatred.[38]

[34] I *in Ps* 139.3.
[35] *Pr* 38.
[36] *Pr* 74.
[37] *M.c.* 42.
[38] *Ep* 27, 6 (in Greek).

Acedia, therefore, has a characteristic Janus head, which clarifies its partially contradictory manifestations, which we will study more precisely later on. *Frustration* and *aggressiveness* combine in a new way and produce this "complex" (that is, interwoven) phenomenon of acedia. It is its very "complexity" that makes it so impenetrable for the affected one, who really feels that he is a "poor animal."

Finally, a characteristic time factor may be added. The other thoughts come and go, at times even very rapidly, for example those of impurity and blasphemy.[39] In contrast, the thought of acedia, because of its complex nature, which unites in itself the most diverse other thoughts, has the characteristic of lasting for a long time. From that duration arises an entirely particular state of mind, such as is typical for depression. When it is not recognized in a timely manner, or rather when one refrains from applying the appropriate remedies, it can become more or less manifest as a permanent condition.

In the life of the soul, acedia thus represents a type of dead end. A distaste for all that is available combined with a diffuse longing for what is not available paralyzes the natural functions of the soul to such a degree that no single one of any of the other thoughts can gain the upper hand!

The text quoted above indicates this complexity, and we again find another important feature. Slackness of soul, characteristic of despondency, is the result of the failure to function in accordance with creation on the part of *both* powers of the soul, desire and anger. This is what Evagrius probably means when he says: "*That means, a slackness of the soul which is not in possession of what is natural, and does not bravely resist the temptations.*"[40]

*

The proper working of the three powers of the soul in accordance with nature and creation, which Evagrius borrowed from Platonic philosophy through his teacher Gregory of Nazianzus, is defined in the following manner:

[39] *Pr* 51.
[40] *O. sp.* 6, 1.

The intelligent soul works in accordance with nature when its desiring part strives after virtue, the irascible does battle for it, and the mental devotes itself to a contemplation of the created.[41]

The three faculties of the soul are intimately related to one another, and all together they have one aim: our blessedness, which consists in the knowledge, first of creation, then of God himself. The natural task of anger is to fight for a pleasure, which desire perceives.[42] The natural urge of desire and anger in accordance with creation is calculated to offer the spiritual delight of knowledge; but this blessing can become distorted and be driven into frustrating worldly desires.

The consequence is that the intellect becomes "darkened," and the knowledge toward which it is aimed can be lost.[43] Its specific sin is therefore "ignorance,"[44] which can be healed only by the knowledge[45] to which spiritual love leads.[46] The full healing of all three powers of the soul and the return to natural functioning in accordance with creation is what Evagrius calls "passionlessness" (*apatheia*). Evagrius describes this state of perfect harmony or "health of the soul"[47] very beautifully in these words:

The one whose mind is always with the Lord and whose incensive part [of the soul] is full of humility through remembrance of God, and whose entire desire is inclined to the Lord, has no need to be afraid of our enemies who encircle our body on the outside.[48]

Desire, anger, and reason are directed toward God in a single impulse and in this way are fully united with one another. When each of these powers goes its own way, then the human being becomes susceptible to adversaries. Again following his teacher Gregory of

[41]*Pr* 86.
[42]*Pr* 24.
[43]*Pr* 24.
[44]*KG* I, 84.
[45]*KG* III, 35.
[46]*KG* III, 58.
[47]*Pr* 56.
[48]*KG* IV, 73.

Nazianzus, Evagrius describes the characteristics of such a soul healed from "the ground up" as follows:

> When virtue finds itself in the mental part [of the soul], it is called circumspection, insight, and wisdom. When it is in the desiring part, it is called discretion, love, and temperance; in the incensive part, courage and patience.[49]

Later we will meet these virtues again and consider their particular role in the struggle with despondency.

*

When we look back at what has been said up to now, it becomes clear in what the complex nature of despondency consists: it is the tangible expression of a deep-seated inner *disintegration* of the human personality as a consequence of sin. For this reason, Evagrius in one place describes despondency strikingly with these words:

> While the other demons, like the rising or setting sun, affect only one part of the soul, the "noonday demon" is in the habit of embracing the entire soul and of suffocating the intellect.[50]

This "suffocating" of the intellect, which is in fact where the image of God and the capacity for God are found—in other words, the *person*—indicates quite clearly the psychological effect of despondency. Like a bell-jar it spreads out over all of life's functions, and it cuts off, so to speak, the vital air one needs for living. "I can't breathe," one says even today in such situations.

As described, acedia is undoubtedly a real vice, from which a human being admittedly suffers, but for which he himself carries the blame—it is a *passion*. Here one may perhaps raise an objection, that this hardly fits melancholy; melancholy may rather be traced to a personal tendency. It is not infrequently conditioned by heredity and is thereby a "destiny," something fated, which man has to bear without having to blame himself for it.[51] Let us attempt to study this in

---

[49] *Pr* 89. As to the questions raised by the shape of the text, see our commentary.
[50] *Pr* 36.
[51] See the "constitutional sorrow" of Guardini in the text cited above, p. 27, note

somewhat greater depth, because the question is not without significance.

*

Although Evagrius did not have at his disposal the insights of modern depth psychology, and his approach to the "suffering of the soul" is altogether fundamentally different, it was not unknown to him that "thoughts" in a certain sense are something prior, with which a man has to come to grips.

> Whether all these [thoughts] disturb the soul or do not disturb the soul does not depend on us.[52]

All passions come into being from a faulty attitude of both the irrational powers of the soul, desire and anger, from which they "arise," as it were, and "darken"[53] the intellect, the core of the human being's person and character. We have already seen that Evagrius reduces the "thoughts," which approach us in the form of temptations, to the working of "demons." However, such temptations would be ineffective if on our side this were never hatched by "*a certain inhuman lust, born of free will, and urging the mind to misuse God's creatures.*"[54] Things in creation are good in themselves since they were called into being by a good Creator. It is *misuse* that makes them "evil,"[55] and the consent of the free will makes mere "thoughts" into sin.[56] For "*whether these thoughts linger or do not linger, excite passions or do not arouse passions, that depends on us.*"[57]

As strongly as Evagrius holds the free will responsible for the origin of evil in the human being, so as to secure personal responsibility from any type of determinism, it has not escaped him that there is one last irrational root which seems to elude one's grasp purely and simply as prior to all:

53, and the 17 selected texts from Kierkegaard, which he uses as the starting point of his own reflections.

[52]*Pr* 6.
[53]*Pr* 74.
[54]*M.c.* 19.
[55]*KG* III, 59.
[56]*Pr* 75.
[57]*Pr* 6.

Alas, this love of self (*philautia*), this "one who hates all."[58]

In "tenderness for oneself" (Irénée Hausherr), Evagrius recognizes the basic substance out of which every passion is made. A passion, quintessentially, is a selfish distortion, a being dominated by one's own self. In all things, it seeks only itself, and in everything, it loves only itself. Since it is not capable of achieving anything by itself, it turns this love of self into a blind hatred of everything.

Why must it be this way? Because there is only one good, eternal desire (*pothos*) that is linked essentially to the intellect: the *desire for true knowledge*,[59] which is focused solely on God and delights the intellect.[60] If this good and eternal desire misses its aim, only sorrow and hatred remain. As the embodiment of all the other passions, acedia is perhaps the purest and "most spiritual" expression of Adam's love of self, which, turned away from God and interested only in himself, ultimately fails even himself.

Thus, they stand in sharp contrast to one another: on the one side, the *totally irrational domain*, which is represented by both powers of the soul, namely, desire and anger (the part "capable of passion"). Here belong the passions as an expression of self-love as well as the demons that stir up evil. On the other side is the "intellect," the core of the human person, which as "image of God"[61] is linked to God by nature. Between the two stands free will, the consent or refusal when confronted by any temptation to evil.

Evil is not able to penetrate man more than God allows and man makes room for it.[62] Meanwhile, Evagrius has no illusions about its might; the temptation of impurity, for instance, can be so strong that man falls into despondency from grieving over its being unbearable.[63] But even here the free will comes in! It decides—despite appearances—against evil and for the good, entirely like Job, the great example of all those who are tempted. Evil remains what it essentially is:

[58] *Sent* 48.
[59] *KG* IV, 50.
[60] *KG* III, 64.
[61] *M.c.* 19.
[62] *Ep* 28, 3.
[63] *Amt* II, 12.

an alien, secondary element, like an illness compared to health,[64] and thereby also finite, limited in time.[65] "For it is possible, then, to be freed entirely from evil!"[66]

*

This unambiguous decision against the irrational and for the *logos* (reason) signifies neither a condemnation nor a suppression of the irrational! For, in the first place, God did not create anything evil *in se* (in itself);[67] it is at most temporary, and passes as soon as its role is fulfilled. In the second place, the entire subtle psychopathology addressed in the ascetical writings of Evagrius teaches that repression is out of the question. Certainly this glance into the "abysses of Satan"[68] is free from any fascination for evil; it is of the greatest soberness. The glance is necessary, nothing more.

This straightforward declaration for the *logos* (reason), however, removes from the battle against evil every tragedy (understood in the ancient sense), which in modern thought once again breaks through powerfully. It points to the last invulnerability of the core of one's being, an invulnerability that flows from the absoluteness of God and of the good. Evagrius can risk taking up the ancient ideal of *apatheia*, of "passionlessness," even that of the true "gnostic" as the perfect man, and fill it with Christian content.[69]

Apatheia to Evagrius is not the goal of asceticism, and the gnostic is more than one who is self-sufficient. *Apatheia* is the indispensable prerequisite for releasing that power which alone grants access to the Person of God: Christian love (*agapē*). The gnostic is one who, through grace, has found this access and who, "face to face," experiences the blessedness that results only from knowledge of God, from the direct dialogue between the "Thou" of God and the "I" of the created spirit, which is indeed his image.

[64]*KG* I, 41.
[65]*KG* I, 40.
[66]*Ep* 43, 2.
[67]*KG* III, 59.
[68]*Off* 2, 24.
[69]See G. Bunge, *Briefe*, 118ff, *id.*, *Geistliche Vaterschaft*.

On this way to God, acedia is the most dangerous opponent, because it threatens to *suffocate* the intellect, the core of the human being. Nevertheless, the human being remains free! He can assent or refuse, which does not prevent the evil one from taking everything, as he did from Job, yes, even nearly his life. But the one who does not assent will, like Job, "see God in this skin."[70] How this is possible, we shall see.

---

[70] *Ep* 1, 2.

CHAPTER 4

Manifestations of Despondency

T he features of despondency are ultimately just as numerous and multiform as our individual frustrations and aggressions. The descriptions Evagrius offers in several of his works, are, accordingly, exceedingly numerous. At every turn they betray his own concrete life circumstances and those of his readers. But one does not need a special astuteness to recognize the general human background in these scenes as tied to time and space—sometimes humorous sketches, occasionally almost caricatures of the monastic and eremitical life.

Many of these caricatures will inevitably provoke the reader to laughter, and that is precisely their significance! For the one who laughs knows that he has been caught and has thereby recognized his own weakness. Recognition is absolutely necessary if one does not want to deal one's blows blindly, as during the night.[1] The following succinct list may offer a first impression of the multiplicity of the manifestations of this evil. Some features of this caricature will be found in this chapter in a more detailed form and will find further clarification there.

> Despondency:
>> breezy love,
> tramper of steps,
>>> hater of love of work,
> fight against solitude,
>>> thunderstorm of psalmody,
> aversion to prayer,
>>> slackening of asceticism,

[1] *Pr* 83.

ill-timed slumber,
 sleep, tossing and turning,
burden of solitude,
 hatred of the cell,
adversary of ascetical efforts,
 counter-attack against endurance,
impediment to reflection,
 ignorance of the Scriptures,
companion of sadness,
 daily rhythm of hunger.[2]

*

"Despondency is a slackness of the soul," Evagrius said, and we have seen earlier that this evil is marked above all by its contradictory character. Everything that is available is hateful to it; everything that is unavailable is desirable. From this inner slackness, as well as from the inconstancy of the soul's movements, many concrete manifestations of despondency are produced, and it is essential to diagnose them precisely, since at first sight they frequently do not allow themselves to be recognized as negative. For the complex character of despondency frequently presents itself under an entirely different raiment, and it seizes all conceivable pretexts not to be recognized as what it really is.

Serious human beings find it endlessly difficult to admit to themselves, and to others who have a need to know, that they suffer from acedia. Important reasons must be furnished to clarify and justify their desolate condition, preferably external circumstances entirely independent of themselves, whose innocent victims they are, against their will. No limits are set to the variations of the illusions, deceptions, and delusions, no different today than in the time of Evagrius. Only the pretexts, which we think up for ourselves, may change with time and circumstances, but basically only the names we ascribe to them have changed.

In what follows, the various manifestations of despondency are presented in ascending order as they emerge from the wide-ranging

---

[2] *Vit* 6.

works of Evagrius. Neither Evagrius nor his interpreter strives for any kind of completeness, which is neither possible nor meaningful. The reader who attentively follows the source reference will observe that Evagrius puts differing accents on his various representations. The great psychologist adapts himself to the capability of his readers, whom we unfortunately no longer know.

> A vagrant monk
>> is dry brushwood in the desert.
> He takes a little rest,
>> and against his will he is once more roaming around.[3]

The first and surest indication of despondency is a certain *inner restlessness*, which can manifest itself in totally different ways. One can no more stand the ancestral home, the work skills acquired, the company of one's friends and acquaintances . . . it is impossible to finish a task begun, to read a book to the end . . . one picks up something and puts it down again . . . one frequently is not aware of what is happening. Plausible reasons appear which ostensibly compel us to "change ourselves."

> For the voluptuary,
>> one woman alone does not suffice,
> And for the despondent monk,
>> a single cell is not enough.[4]

On the thought of despondency that takes great pains in finding another cell to live in, while the first which he possessed has become entirely hated and full of dampness; diseases of all sorts have resulted from this . . . [5]

Evagrius repeatedly mentions the temptation to *move*[6] since it is typical of anchorites, for obvious reasons. The hermit lives year in and year out in the same self-willed isolation of his four walls, and thereby

[3] *O. sp.* 6, 10.
[4] *O. sp.* 6, 13.
[5] *Ant* IV, 26.
[6] *Ant* VI, 33, 52, 57; *Mn* 55; *Ep* 27, 2; *M.c.* 11.

does without all the little daily changes, which for one living in the "world" disguise how much he has been assailed by the vice of restlessness.

"Sitting" (in the cell) is so characteristic of the monastic life that the expression became a synonym for "being a monk" until well into the western Middle Ages. The temptation of bodily vagabondage is the tangible manifestation of that fundamental evil which undermines any spiritual life: the vagabondage of thoughts. The anchorite therefore settles his body in his cell and his thoughts in remembering God. This is the true *stabilitas loci* (stability of place) to which Benedict attaches great importance.

The subterfuges for giving up one's place of residence vary from person to person: the anchorite will lay out for himself different ones than the Christian living in the world. Viewed objectively, they may seem perfectly justified, but in an insidious manner they appear convincing to us only when we suffer from despondency.

Naturally, this restlessness can make use of more subtle arguments, as for instance, the dampness of the cell; so, for example, the cunning observation:

> Pleasing God is not bound to a place. They say that God can be adored everywhere.[7]

Who would want to deny this? But did our anchorite not move into the desert precisely in order to adore God undisturbed by all worldly business? At the same time, Evagrius is not altogether in principle against a change of place; on the contrary, he proves himself to be more flexible than many other desert fathers. In passing he once mentions some serious reasons that oblige one to leave one's present residence: when the cell proves to be all too easily accessible and no longer guarantees the seclusion needed. In this case, one will not hold on to one's living place through a false attachment![8] Not to want to depart in spite of the inappropriateness of the living place would then be nothing more than a certain sign of vainglory![9]

[7]*Pr* 12.
[8]*R. m.* 5.
[9]*Ant* VII, 21.

In case of doubt, one should ask for advice, as Palladius did once when acedia had evidently caused him a lot of bother:

> One day I went to [Macarius of Alexandria, the spiritual father of the Kellia (cells)], as I suffered from despondency; and I said to him: "Abba, what shall I do? For the thoughts besiege me and say: You do nothing! Go away from there!" And he said to me: "Tell them, 'I guard these walls [of my cell] because of the will of Christ!' "[10]

We encounter these doubts concerning the ascetical life frequently. Palladius bravely resisted them for a while. After the death of his teacher, however, he left the desert. Upon basic complaints about his health, the doctors recommended to him a change of climate: his spleen and stomach seemed affected.[11] Significantly, his poor health apparently did not cause him any further difficulties during his truly eventful career as a bishop, nor during his slef-imposed exile in Egypt, which lasted for years . . .

*

At the same time, Palladius knew the spiritual teaching of his instructor accurately, and he realized that the worry about bodily health was all too often only a temptation of acedia.

> On the thought of despondency which projects for us prolonged old age, and bitter, uncomforted poverty, and a disease that is able to kill the body . . . [12]

> On the soul, which picks up thoughts of despondency because of an illness of the body . . . [13]

This fear of falling ill, which Evagrius, in a chapter on gluttony in the *Praktikos*, depicts in a particularly colorful way, was not in itself entirely groundless: stomach, liver, spleen, dropsy, a long illness, a lack of the most essential things, no physician within reach—all these pass

---

[10]*HL* 18: Butler.
[11]*HL* 35: Butler.
[12]*Ant* VI, 32.
[13]*Ant* VI, 36.

before the spiritual eye of the anchorite.[14] In the desert, certainly
there was often a lack of what was most necessary. But, for the monk,
a disease means a request, a thanksgiving for the pains, and learning
patience with the brethren who serve us. But the demons seek to
hamper us with anxieties,[15] while at the time of despondency they
depict for us all manner of diseases to endure.

Furthermore, the secret connection between psychic and physical
diseases, of such concern to modern medicine, was known perfectly
well to Evagrius. In the *Antirrhētikos*, in the chapter on sadness,[16]
which certainly is linked most intimately to despondency,[17] he
describes quite astonishing psychosomatic phenomena that tend to
appear as the result of extreme states of anxiety. A modern psychiatrist
would accept them today. A great deal could be added concerning
dreadful nightmares, demonic apparitions, and so forth. Let it suffice
for us to have made reference to these worrisome manifestations,
resulting from sadness, which were also well known to the ancients.

*

There are other harmless manifestations of despondency that, at first
sight, do not reveal themselves as such.

> On the thoughts of the demon of despondency who hates the man-
> ual labor of the occupation he practices; he hates it and wants to
> learn another occupation that will support himself better and cause
> less trouble . . . [18]

The temptation suddenly to view one's work or learned profession
as the source of one's indisposition must have been widespread in
Evagrius' time; at any rate, he makes mention of it in several places.[19]
Today it might be as common as at that time, and for the same reasons. The monks of old earned their keep mostly by weaving bas-

---

[14]*Pr* 7.
[15]*Pr* 40.
[16]*Ant* IV.
[17]See *Ant* IV, 35, 37.
[18]*Ant* VI, 1.
[19]*Ant* VI, 33; *O. sp.* 6, 12.

kets—a simple, almost mechanical task, which in the long run must have been dreadfully monotonous. Such monotony was nonetheless consciously searched for, because under normal conditions it left the spirit free for prayer and contemplation, and indeed directly called for such spiritual activity. But when a monk falls into despondency, then the quality of this work turns into its opposite, and the work itself becomes a heavy burden. We will frequently come across this reverse side of special and originally beneficial qualities of life in the desert: loneliness, silence, renunciation of the life of luxury.

The same experience may be thoroughly familiar to modern people. With all the means of technology one's daily burden of work lessens, thus freeing one for something else. But in simplification lies the danger of spirit-killing routine and monotony. If the person for any reason falls into despondency, then this "freedom for something else" suddenly appears as an empty word and the daily work itself as a source of discontent. All too often this is a fatal illusion. To the one who is filled inwardly, monotonous work progresses rapidly, almost unconsciously. He is really free for "something else."

*

Instead of his handiwork, there can also be "superiors" or "colleagues," in short, fellow human beings upon whom we lay the guilt of our misfortune. The despondent one suddenly remembers in painful detail all the injustices he has had to put up with, either in reality or in his imagination.[20]

> On the thought, which through despondency encourages slander against the monastic superior on the pretext that he allegedly does not strengthen the brethren and is harsh with them and has no compassion for them in their distress . . . [21]

One can judge by the number of examples Evagrius gives that this temptation must have been quite frequent.[22] The temptation lies particularly close since we are nowhere else so vulnerable as in the so-

[20]*Pr* 12.
[21]*Ant* VI, 2.
[22]*Ant* VI, 13, 30, 48, 55.

called affective domain. This is why Evagrius strikingly says of the despondent one, that this thought is painful to him: that *love among the brethren has vanished, and no one is found to comfort him.*[23]

Above all, unmarried people, monks, or celibate priests, easily yield to the illusion that the source of their unhappiness is their unmarried state, their lack of truly human attachment. But does a married person in such a situation not experience exactly the same in his relationship to the wedded partner, or indeed to any person in his relationships with them? Deception and self-delusion have led many astray while the true character of their depression remains hidden. They do not understand that they are entangled in the most unusual *struggle with themselves* and that their opponent is neither "the institution," nor "a vow," nor the marriage partner or colleagues at work, or whatever, but their own wounded "I." The root of all evil is that "love of self" to which Evagrius reduces all eight generic "thoughts."

*

From time immemorial there has been, after all, a proven means to escape from the burden of despondency—distraction and amusement!

> On the thought that irritates us at the time of despondency to go to the brethren, in order to be comforted by them . . . [24]

> To the Lord, on the thoughts of despondency, which make our patience waver and irritate us, to have a little rest and to see once again our house and our relatives after a long time . . . [25]

An entire entertainment and travel industry is occupied today with just this: to lighten the burden of despondency for our poor contemporaries, or rather, to prevent them even from realizing that they are afflicted with this evil. There must be no standing still, no emptiness! "Grief shared is grief halved," and the beneficial effects of a trip, of a "change of scene," are they not known from of old? But the evil is not remedied by this, only postponed. The beautiful illusion vanishes and despondency returns and requires yet stronger doses.

[23]*Pr* 12.
[24]*Ant* VI, 24.
[25]*Ant* VI, 39.

The yearning so characteristic of despondency for diverse amusements in general, and especially for human companionship, can become almost overwhelming.

> On the intellect which is buffeted on all sides by thoughts of despondency, and is now driven by anger from [its] location, now pulled away by the throat to another place, to the brothers or to his relatives and the world, which formerly and oftentimes humiliated and demeaned him . . . [26]

As the condition continues, it eventually assumes a form of nervous exhaustion. The texts that follow expose this mercilessly. The end of the chapter of the *Antirrhetikos* makes clear that the "victim" always acts against his better judgment. But the urge to seek refuge among fellow human beings from the burden of despondency grabs the poor one literally by the throat . . .

Does this mean that one should avoid human relationships as far as lies in one's power? Anything but that! From the *Apophthegmata* and also from the writings of Evagrius we know that the desert fathers visited one another gladly and frequently, above all to get advice from an older and more experienced monk. Not to do this is in fact a sign of spiritual pride.

> On the arrogant thought that hinders me from seeing the brothers, since they too supposedly have no greater insight than I have . . . [27]

As the little episode from the life of Palladius quoted above teaches us, such a visit to an experienced spiritual father in case of despondency is not only allowed, but even a commandment of meekness and prudence. Frequently one does not see clearly on one's own. Antony, who was left entirely to his own devices, even needed the visit of an angel, who showed him a way out of his difficult situation.

*

As a true vice, despondency especially likes to disguise itself as virtue in circumstances where its ugly face would spread only disgust and

[26] *Ant* VI, 57.
[27] *Ant* VIII, 33.

terror. For who enjoys being in the company of a despondent fellow
human being?

> Visits to the sick
>   the despondent one uses as a pretext.
> But in fact he satisfies
>   only his own goal.[28]
> A despondent monk
>   is quick to help,
> and considers his own gratification
>   to be a command.[29]

Restlessness changes into a busy, untiring activism and sees itself
as the Christian virtue of brotherly love! But it is nothing more than
an illusion, a dangerous self-deception. It is the illusion of a full
appointments calendar that blinds us to our inner emptiness. It is all
the more dangerous as it serves so-called high goals and is therefore
unassailable. The longer this illusion continues, the more disastrous
the consequences. The sudden end of the delusion, the dreadful
awakening, inevitably comes sooner or later. One will either give up
in desperation, dropping everything that up to then had ostensibly
made up the content of life, or one will clutch at new and ever
stronger doses of distraction.

How much knowledge of the heart and *discernment of spirits* are
needed here to distinguish truth from appearance! The demon is
indeed a friend of every type of exaggeration, as we shall see.

Meanwhile, there is a safe criterion to distinguish real love of
neighbor, which for Evagrius always manifests itself as meekness,
from its counterfeit: its fruits. True love makes one lovable; by contrast, "charitable activism," born from despondency, renders one bit-
ter and intolerant.

The following sketch, in which Evagrius describes, not without
humor, the grotesque forms despondency eventually assumes, has
rightly become famous:

[28] *O. sp.* 6, 6.
[29] *O. sp.* 6, 7.

The eye of the despondent one
    stares constantly at the window,
and his mind
    presents visitors to him.
The door creaks,
    and he jumps up;
he hears a voice,
    and peers through the window,
and he does not go away from there,
    until, exhausted, he sits down.
If the despondent one reads,
    then he yawns a great deal,
    and soon he sinks into sleep.
He rubs his eyes,
    and stretches out his hands,
and while his eyes wander from the book,
    he stares at the wall,
then he turns away again,
    and reads a little,
and when he leafs through [the book],
    he searches for the end of the exposition.
He counts the pages,
    and determines the number of sheets,
finds fault with the writing and the design
    and in the end he snaps the book shut.
He lays his head on it,
    and falls into a not-too-deep sleep,
and in the end hunger
    wakes up the soul again, and the soul [now renewed]
attends to its own concerns.[30]

A similar caricature of a poor victim of despondency, this time tailored especially to the eremitical life, is found in the *Praktikos*, a true synthesis of all the conceivable symptoms of this vice. We have already quoted some individual lines; here follows the entire text in its context:

[30] *O. sp.* 6, 14–15.

The demon of despondency (acedia), also called the "noonday demon," is the most oppressive one. He attacks the monk at the fourth hour, and circles around his soul until the eighth hour.

First of all, looking at the sun, [the monk] concludes that the sun hardly moves or does not move at all, and he has the impression that the day is fifty hours long.

Then the demon compels the monk to look constantly out of the window, and to jump out of his cell, to observe the sun, how far it is removed from the ninth hour, and he looks now this way and then that way to see if one of the brethren [appears from his cell].

Further, [the demon] instills in the monk a hatred for his place, his life [as a monk], and his manual labor, and [he whispers to him] that charity among the brethren has disappeared, and that he finds no one to console him. And if anyone has recently offended the monk, the demon also attends to this, in order to increase his hatred.

The demon leads him to long for other places, where one could easily find [life's] necessities, and where he could take up a lighter and more profitable occupation. To this, [the demon] adds that pleasing God is not linked to one place, and that one can adore God everywhere.

The demon joins to this the remembrance of the monk's relatives and his earlier life. He describes to the monk how long life is, and brings before his eyes the toils of asceticism. He sets in motion against the monk, as it were, all his siege engines, in order to force the monk [if possible] to give up his cell and flee from the arena.

No other demon follows closely upon this one. After the struggle, the soul is in a sure state of deep peace, and an ineffable joy.[31]

The description is unmistakably tailored to a certain way of life: the lonely life of an anchorite in his desert cell. The long fast until 3:00 p.m. allows despondency on account of the daily rhythm of hunger, as we read at the beginning. Rarely encountering others creates a feeling of total abandonment, and who would be astonished that a lonely place of residence and monotonous work cause the monk to wish for change? What could be more understandable than melan-

[31]*Pr* 12.

choly for the security of his own family, which the ascetic has left once and for all? And yet, we look into this particular situation from the inside, in order to recognize in this extreme situation the fundamental vulnerability of the human being. Few will have read the two preceding chapters without dismay. But worse is yet to come!

*

Acedia has devastating consequences above all on the *life of prayer*. How could it be otherwise? The general sluggishness despondency spreads has the logical effect of causing negligence and laziness in celebrating the Office.[32]

> A despondent monk,
> is dilatory at prayer.
> And at times, he does not
> speak the words of the prayer at all.
> Then, just as a sick person carries no heavy burden,
> so the despondent monk never, at any time,
> performs
> the work of God with care.
> The sick person, indeed,
> has lost the strength of life,
> while in the monk, by contrast,
> the resilience of his soul has gone slack.[33]

The Egyptian monks of the early period devoted themselves in the daytime—and also during a good part of the night—to light manual labor to promote concentration of the mind. This was interrupted at regular intervals by "meditation," that is, by a meditative repetition of biblical passages learned by heart, and by prayer. Indeed, the aim of the monastic life is "constant and uninterrupted perseverance in prayer,"[34] a state which in its highest form is "a dialogue of the intel-

---

[32]For what follows, see G. Bunge, *Geistgebet*, Ch. II ("Pray without Ceasing") and V (The Condition of Prayer).

[33]*O. sp.* 6, 16.

[34]Cassian, *Conf* IX, 2. [For an English version, see John Cassian, *The Conferences*, Boniface Ramsey, tr. (New York: Paulist Press, 1997)].

lect with God, with no intermediary."[35] When the monk falls into despondency, this desired aim suddenly becomes an unbearable burden.

In addition, at the beginning and the end of night, the monks celebrated two "synaxes" (Offices) of twelve psalms each, with every psalm followed by a freely formulated personal prayer.[36] These "little synaxes," as the monks themselves called them, were not particularly demanding, except for the one who suffered from despondency.

> Sometimes, when acedia encompasses the soul, [the demon] suggests to us that we [only move the tongue in the mouth]; sometimes he incites us to sing what is to be recited, and precisely when the soul is infested with self-satisfaction. In particular, the demon of despondency creates listlessness when one rises for prayer. Then he bothers us again when we pray or psalmodize, in that he urges us to hurry.[37]

This same listlessness appears when it is a question of learning by heart the scriptural texts used during meditation, as was customary among the early monks.

> On the thought of despondency, which turns us away from the reading [of Holy Scripture] and from the study of spiritual words, in that it asserts: "Look, that certain holy old man knew only twelve psalms, and [yet] he was pleasing to God!"[38]

Therefore, a typical temptation of acedia is minimalism in prayer, and one is not at a loss for rationalizations. Who has not heard the so plausible argument that it is impossible to "complete" the many psalms of the Office? Evagrius diagnoses here a symptom of despondency, for "as long as the spirit of despondency weighs heavily on you, it convinces the soul that psalmody is oppressive, and it casts reluc-

[35] *Or* 3.

[36] See G. Bunge, *Irdene Gefässe. Die Praxis des persönliches Gebetes der heiligen Väter, Würzburg* (1996). [In English, *Earthen Vessels; The Practice of Personal Prayer According to the Patristic Tradition*, Michael J. Miller, tr. (San Francisco: Ignatius Press, 2002)].

[37] *Eul* 9.

[38] *Ant* VI, 5.

tance as an adversary against the soul."[39] For how many monastics have the apparently so intelligible, psychologically so understandable arguments of acedia, continually spoiled joy at prayer and at the Office? One has to be especially careful, for the death of one's prayer life is the death of the spiritual life in general.

*

For many of the faithful, things will not go any better whether they attend church or not. Each person finds himself in a state of mind where everything is "too much," all the little household or professional obligations, which he used to carry out with ease. He finds himself, so to speak, without air, as if he were running to catch a train that is leaving. Who is conscious that he is a victim of despondency?

Not entirely unjustly, one may perhaps raise the objection that this feeling of being overburdened is well-founded. This was not unknown to the ancients. Evagrius is anything but an uncompromising maximalist or an apprehensive, scrupulous man.

Thus we find in him the noteworthy warning, which casts a bright light on the true meaning of ascetical monasticism, against committing oneself by oath to certain "achievements." Such exaggerations are from the evil one and altogether alien to the true nature of monasticism![40]

*

In the background, there thus stands an experience which is at first glance astonishing. The adversary not only talks us into a lukewarm minimalism, but also drives us, on occasion, to a destructive maximalism! In an insidious fashion, he changes position and jumps into being an advocate of the highest virtue.

> But the opponent of truth, the demon of acedia also mimics this one
> [namely, the demon of gluttony] inasmuch as he advises the stead-
> fast [monk] to an extreme withdrawal whereby he appeals to the
> emulation of John the Baptist, and the first of anchorites, Antony,

[39] *Eul* 9.
[40] *Ant* I, 27.

so that, when [the monk] fails to endure the long and superhuman withdrawal, he takes to flight with dishonor, leaves the place, and the demon then says in triumph:[41] "*I have prevailed over him!*"[42]

We cannot marvel enough at the fine sense of distinction with which Evagrius, in an environment which apparently was organized for maximum ascetical efficiency, knew how to separate truth from demonic deception. Another text, in which he describes how the demons always impel us to what is most harmful at the moment, teaches us how clear it was for him, and no mere passing insight:

> [The demons] hinder the sick from saying thanks for their pains, and from forbearance towards their servants. Instead of this, they urge the exhausted to be abstinent and the down-hearted to psalmodize standing up.[43]

Later still, we shall see to whom Evagrius is indebted for such a fine sense of due proportion in everything. Evagrius shows himself a trustworthy witness to the best monastic tradition.

The same temptation to exaggerate by excess in doing good may also stand behind a beautiful text which we will quote at length later on.[44] Here Evagrius does not enter into the deeper causes of despondency; as its immediate reason, he mentions only the effort that is linked to the spiritual life. But since effort must be made with moderation, one may presume that "Jacob," while "guarding the sheep" day and night, overtaxed his powers a little.[45]

*

The texts quoted above teach that in the spiritual life one may not be satisfied with superficial judgments. Despondency is a deep-seated evil, one that disguises its true nature as far as possible. Thus one instinctively demands to know: how is it possible to distinguish true motives from false?

[41]See Ps 12.5.
[42]*M.c.* 35.
[43]*Pr* 40.
[44]*M.c.* 17. See the beginning of chapter 6.
[45]The reference is to Jacob's reproach to Laban in Gen 31.39–40.

In his *Letters*, Evagrius deals with this question at length. As a criterion of distinction he mentions the intention with which we do or refrain from doing something. In other words, it is a matter of whether we want to do good for its own sake, or whether we pursue self-seeking aims.[46] Self-seeking in all its manifestations is no different from the "love of self" that lies at the root of all vice.

Meanwhile the demon is able to trap us, in that he sets "snares on the straight path." To an intention that is good in itself he attaches an egoistic goal. Evagrius solves this apparent dilemma, in that he advises, simply, to hold courageously to the first good intention, for the Holy Spirit knows well that it is impossible for a human being, in the struggle with the demons, to maintain his hold on to a good idea unchallenged.

The same thing works in the opposite direction. Our evil intentions we are not able to hold out "untempted" either, since "seeds of virtue," indestructible in themselves, which God sank deeply into the soil of our nature at our creation, do not allow this.[47]

In this characteristic interplay, whereby "the thoughts divide and are divided, that is, the good ones divide the bad, and are divided again by them,"[48] the free human person develops. The ground of our nature is good, *"for we were not evil in the beginning, since the sower, who is our Lord, sowed good seed in his field."* [49] From this good soil proceed the good impulses, common to all human beings.[50] The angels promote this good through good inspirations, while the demons put it to the test by evil ones. It depends on our will, its willingness or its carelessness, which way we are ultimately inclined. But a free will means being a responsible person.

But let us return to the manifestations of despondency.

*

[46]See *Pr Prol* [3].
[47]*Ep* 17 and 18.
[48]*Ep* 18, 3.
[49]*Ep* 18, 2; see Mt 13.27.
[50]*Ep* 18, 1.

In the event the anchorite has, after all this, still not left his cell, then despondency provokes a condition of general discouragement.

> On the soul that picks up thoughts from despondency, which cut off hope, in that they demonstrate that the anchorite's life is very hard and hardly anyone can bear its mode of life ... [51]

It is easy to guess where this discouragement will lead when it lasts a long time. Is it any wonder if the unfortunate victim comes, after a while, to doubt the meaning of the monastic life?

> On the thought that then maintains that it is possible, without monasticism, to acquire purity and a [sound] state of health [of the soul] ... [52]

Who has not heard that peculiar modern "encouraging" argument, relating not only to the monastic life but, according to circumstances, to everything opposed to our best inclinations? But there is worse to come. Theoretical doubts about the meaning of monastic life radically call into question one's own vocation when one gives way to them.

> On the thoughts of despondency that arise in us because our relatives claim that we have left the world and fallen in love with monasticism not because of God's will, but either because of our sins or because of our weakness, on account of which we are in no condition to deal with the affairs of the world like a man ... [53]

In the end, the poor man has nothing else in mind than to hang his cowl on its hook as quickly as possible and "leave the arena."[54]

> On the thoughts of the soul that through despondency begin to waver and abandon the holy path of the brave and one's dwelling ...[55]

[51]*Ant* VI, 14.
[52]*Ant* VI, 41.
[53]*Ant* VI, 46.
[54]*Pr* 12.
[55]*Ant* VI, 52.

No one will maintain that such thoughts come only to anchorites. We cannot admire sufficiently the perspicacity with which Evagrius unmasks as a temptation of acedia all secret doubt about the authenticity of one's calling, of one's decision to follow a certain type of life, whether it be as monk, priest, or married man. These thoughts infiltrate slowly, and with time they hollow out inner confidence, like water dripping on stone. Considered from the purely human point of view, in every decision, in addition to the high-minded and authentic, there are all types of merely foregrounded and entirely ignoble motives at play. But God writes straight with crooked lines, since he calls sinners, not the righteous. Each "calling" turns out to be, in a retrospect of belief, an ultimately grace-full *election*.

The mysterious interplay of human weakness and divine strength remains forever hidden to hasty unbelief, and for the demon it is an easy thing to make the despondent person believe that what was involved in the game was the human, all too human, but nothing more. Such a fatal illusion, as you see, by which many are taken in—and not for the first time today! How much knowledge of the heart is needed in order to separate what is truly necessary from thousands of delusions!

*

For many reasons, internal and external, it may not be possible for the despondent person to escape from his difficult situation. He may have already used all customary means of diversion and, in the end, ended up again in his customary despondency. Then it may happen that he falls into a deep depression of soul whose morbid features Evagrius describes with disquieting clarity.

> On the soul, which on account of thoughts of slowness and despondency that have lingered in it, has become weak and exhausted and which has faded away in bitterness, and whose strength is consumed by great dejection, and is close to desperation on account of the power of this demon, in so far as the soul rages and behaves like a child with passionate and groaning tears, and for which there is no refreshing breeze anywhere . . . [56]

[56]*Ant* VI, 38.

All this is nothing else but the desperate expression of an ultimate insight that all attempts at escape have proven aimless. *Abyssus abyssum invocat.*[57] The abyss, nothingness itself, calls unto abyss—an empty cry in emptiness.

If this desolate condition lasts too long and suffocates the intellect, the personhood of the human being as Evagrius says,[58] then to someone who is despondent may very well befall what Evagrius gives as the result of sadness, the immediate cause of despondency.

> All demons teach the soul to love pleasure. Only the demon of sadness does not understand how to do this. Rather, he corrupts the thoughts [of the arriving demons][59] in that he cuts off [from them] any pleasure, and through sadness,"the bones of the sad man are dried up."[60]
>
> When he attacks the anchorite moderately, he tries and tests him, and then he convinces him not to accept any of the things of the world and to shun all pleasure. If he lingers on [as despondency], then he plants thoughts which advise the soul to escape [the body] or coerce it to run far away from its present abode. This is also what the saintly Job pondered once and endured, when he was troubled by this demon: "O that I could bring myself to lay hands upon myself, or at least ask someone else to do this for me!"[61]
>
> The symbol of this demon is the viper. This animal's natural power, when one gives a humanly bearable dosage, destroys the poisons of other animals; undiluted, however, it destroys the living being itself.[62]

*

Who would have assumed at the beginning of this chapter that what began as a whimsical discontent could end this way? And yet, Eva-

---

[57]Ps 41.8.

[58]*Pr* 36.

[59]See Sk 61: "Among the thoughts are those of sadness: they only are the ones that destroy all the [others]."

[60]Prov 17.22.

[61]Job 30.24 (LXX).

[62]*M.c.* 12.

grius has seen rightly. *Suicide* is in many cases nothing more than the last desperate attempt at a flight from one's own inner emptiness into nothingness, a "solution to the conflict," which Evagrius by the way explicitly rejects several times.[63]

Under the influence of sorrow at the death of his father, Evagrius cites Psalm 141.10 as a desirable goal: "Bring my soul out of prison that I may confess Thy name."[64] Yet in a different place, he qualifies that this plea is becoming only for the Pure, who are fit for knowledge of creation even without the body.[65] The one who remains in captivity to the passions and asks for this—to be able quickly to leave the body—resembles a sick man who asks a cabinetmaker to smash up his bed as quickly as possible . . .[66]

There is hardly a text in this chapter by which the modern reader does not feel existentially addressed one way or another. Acedia is an omnipresent phenomenon linked to being human. Time, place, and life circumstances change its concrete manifestations, but of its nature, the phenomenon is timeless.

[63] *KG* IV, 33, 76, 83.
[64] *Ep* 56, 1.
[65] *KG* IV, 70.
[66] *KG* IV, 76.

CHAPTER 5

The Remedies

T he unrelenting anatomy of the phenomenon of despondency could well lead many to the mistaken conclusion that the disease is incurable. But that would be a fallacy and basically nothing more than a further illusion of despondency. Like all ancient monasticism and the early church in general regarding the possibility of victory over evil, Evagrius is unshakably optimistic. Evil is fundamentally non-being, a fake, parasitic being. As such, it has been unmasked by Christ, put on display, and deprived of power.[1] The demon has no more power over human beings; though the despondent man, like a fool, comes to belong to him once more. Despondency, this conglomerate of all imaginable vices, for Evagrius is a thoroughly curable disease; indeed, the medication he prescribes is surprisingly simple.

*

The remedies against despondency are of two types: general and specific. Since despondency is an illness of both the irrational powers of the soul—*desire* and *anger*—it is essential to heal both at the root. Since now

> "knowledge and ignorance are linked to the intellect, desire is receptive to temperance and impurity; but love and hatred run up to anger,"[2] "knowledge heals the intellect; love, anger; and abstinence, desire."[3]

[1] 1 Col 2.15.
[2] *KG* I, 84.
[3] *KG* III, 35.

Spiritual love and moderation heal the passions of the soul and the body, it is said at another place.[4] Passions of the soul are by far the most stubborn and pursue the human being until his death; those of the body, on the contrary, withdraw more quickly.[5] Accordingly, this is why anger requires more intensive treatment, on account of which St Paul called love "great."[6] Knowledge, love, which Evagrius defines as meekness,[7] and moderation, these three concepts embrace the entire spiritual life as Evagrius understands it. He learned this from the holy fathers.

> The fear of God strengthens faith, and, in turn, continence; the lat-
> ter makes patience and hope inflexible, from which is born dispas-
> sion, the offshoot of which is love. But love is the gateway to a
> natural knowledge (that is, a knowledge of created natures), upon
> which follows theology [a knowledge of God himself] and eternal
> beatitude.[8]

Dealing with knowledge, love, and temperance would require describing the entire spiritual life in detail, which is impossible within our setting. For us it suffices to state what Evagrius mentions once about sadness, the fatal companion and forerunner of despondency, and its intimate connection to all the remaining vices. More than all others, the text makes clear that in the spiritual life one must begin "from below."

The "below" is the irrational longing which expelled our first parents from Paradise.[9] Also made clear is that without chastity, no love is possible. Spiritual love loves the other for his sake and does not question his integrity. Desire, in contrast, is an egoistic distortion, and since its craving necessarily remains unsatisfied, sadness and despondency always follow it.

A prisoner of the Barbarians
is bound with iron,

[4] *Pr* 35.
[5] *Pr* 36.
[6] *Pr* 38. See 1 Cor 13.13.
[7] See *Ep* 56, 3ff.
[8] *Pr Prol* [8].
[9] *O. sp.* 1, 10.

and a prisoner of the passions
    is bound by sorrow.
Sorrow is powerless
    if the other passions are not at hand,
just as fetters are able to do nothing
    if the fetterers are not present.
The one who is bound by sorrow
    has been besieged [first] by [the other] passions.
And he carries the fetters around with him
    as a proof of his defeat.
Then sorrow results
    from the failure of a fleshly desire;
but a desire
    is linked to each passion.
The one who has vanquished desire
    has defeated the passions.
And the one who has defeated the passions
    will not be dominated by grief.[10]

*

Consequently, if real healing is possible only when evil is eradicated, in daily life what remains is to reach for a specific remedy and to use it where the symptoms of evil become visible. One must start somewhere, and in the case of despondency it is indispensable to use a strong medicine at once, one that promises some immediate success. There are several such specific remedies.

Evagrius has defined despondency as *atonia,* a slackness of soul, and has thereby shown[11] its affinity with cowardice as the common feature of all its manifestations, particularly restlessness or a tendency toward flight. Cowardice is a vice that is the opposite of manliness. We are thereby referred to a text cited earlier in which Evagrius describes the three powers of the soul according to nature and creation. It was said there that the virtues of the irascible power of the soul are courage and patience, whose role Evagrius defines thus:

[10]*O. sp.* 5, 8–11.
[11]See *Pr* 28.

The work of patience and courage is to know no fear of enemies and eagerly to endure afflictions.[12]

Accordingly, since despondency is a form of cowardice, it is important first to counteract this unnatural working of the irascible part of the soul. Evagrius states laconically:

> Patience:
> a crushing of despondency.[13]

So that, through patience, your reward may rain down upon you more abundantly, your patience must make war through all manly virtues, for with the help of each evil, despondency also fights against you and tries you, in that it observes all your efforts. And the one whom it does not find nailed down through patience; it weighs down with itself and keeps him down.[14]

And once more in terse brevity:

> Patience together with tears keeps down despondency.[15]

*

We have already seen that acedia, when it becomes an enduring condition, is not harmless. In an extreme case, it can drive its victim to suicide. Even if it does not get that far, spiritual death still threatens. In the text that follows, Evagrius describes a condition which he calls "hard-heartedness" or "total unconcern" (*anaisthēsia*). He describes it as a direct result of *"prolonged thoughts of vainglory,"* and he writes, in addition: *"if that time had not been shortened, no human being would have survived."*[16] This *spiritual death*, an expression of a complete victory of the demons and of their passions over the soul,[17] easily turns into acedia, as we shall see.

---

[12]*Pr* 89.

[13]*Vit* 6.

[14]*Eul* 8.

[15]*Inst. mon.* I, 5. [For an English version, see *The Twelve Books of John Cassian on the Institutes of the Coenobia* (NPNF-XII 11:201–290)].

[16]Mt 24.22.

[17]*KG* IV, 85.

But what shall one say about the demon that makes the soul unfeeling? I am afraid even to write about him: how the soul at his drawing near falls out of its own state and casts off both the fear of God and piety, no longer considers sin as sin, nor crime as crime, and conceives of punishment and the eternal judgment as if they were a matter of mere words, and quite derides "the earthquake pregnant with fire,"[18] and though he admits God ostensibly, nevertheless he ignores what God has commanded.

You beat your breast, because it has turned to sin, and is not conscious of it. You quote from the Scriptures, but [your heart] is thoroughly hardened and does not listen. You charge [your heart] with opprobrium before men, but it does not even notice its shame before your brothers. In short, [your heart] is completely without insight, like a pig that breaks through a fence with its eyes tightly shut. [19]

In timeless words that require no further comment, Evagrius describes this state, of which he says that it rarely strikes those who live in community. Today one may be less optimistic that this demon is driven away by the sight of the injury inflicted upon others around us, and the remorse and compassion it awakens in us. Modern man is no longer so easily shaken.

How much is at stake in this struggle the conclusion of the quotation teaches us, for it indicates the "reward" of patient perseverance; we will return to this at greater length later on.

Meanwhile, we need to know this: when an anchorite who gets caught by this demon [of insensibility] does not adopt unclean thoughts, or does not leave his house through despondency, then he has received the prudence and patience that descend from heaven, and blessed is the one who is deemed worthy of such passionlessness.

Meanwhile, the one who [as monk] has always praised the fear of God, and plans to live together with worldly people, let him be on his guard against this demon! As far as I am concerned, I feel ashamed even in front of people to speak or write more about him.[20]

[18]Job 41.21 (LXX).
[19]*M.c.* 11.
[20]*Ibid.*, 11.

*

In the face of the intensity with which acedia attacks its victim and, as it were, "seizes him by the throat,"[21] the first and most powerful remedy is therefore sheer *endurance*. In spite of the apparently over-powering temptation to flee, it is necessary to remain "as nailed down."[22] For the anchorite—and not only for him—it means first of all that one holds out until the attack is over.

> At the moment of temptations, one must not leave one's cell, no matter how reasonable may be the excuses which one lays out for oneself. Rather, one must stay inside and sit quietly, and hold out, and meet all attackers with courage, above all the demon of despondency, which is more oppressive than all the others and makes the soul extremely well-tried. For to flee such battles and avoid them teaches the intellect to be inept, cowardly, and a runaway.[23]

Such conduct appears perhaps to many as the downright opposite of what one would normally do in this situation, from a rational point of view. And yet Evagrius gives an account of the outcome of his own experiences and those of many others when he advises not to follow the instinctive urge to flee. Only one's own experience can prove the truth of this advice, which Abba Moses once summarized succinctly:

> Away, enter your cell and sit down, and your cell will teach you everything.[24]

In this sheer endurance of the anchorite in his cell, everything else is included: the conscious renunciation of any type of diversion and distraction, be it in the form of traveling, visits, or conversations. Is there a lack of psychological understanding for the most elementary needs of the human being? Absolutely not. Another monk, whose thoughts tempted him, came to hear from Abba Arsenius this aston-ishing answer, which differentiates in an admirable manner the essen-tial from the non-essential:

[21] *Ant* VI, 57.
[22] *Eul* 8.
[23] *Pr* 28.
[24] *Apophthegm Moses* 6.

Go, eat, drink, sleep, and do not work, only do not leave your cell![25]

As there is a hierarchy of values, so there is also a hierarchy of evil. In the case of despondency, the end and rallying point of the other vices, endurance in isolation is more important than the remaining ascetical exercises. If necessary, one must even "drive out one nail with another," as Evagrius says once,[26] which means in this case to choose the lesser evil—assuming, naturally, that one does not thereby give way to despondency in a secret manner.

Thus, let us refer to the *reward* promised to the one who perseveres! Later we will return to this at length.[27]

> When the spirit of despondency
>   comes over you,
>   then do not leave your house,
>   and at that moment
> do not evade the profitable struggle!
>   Just as one makes silver shiny;
>   so will your heart become radiant.[28]

In order to ease the pressure of despondency a little, relaxation such as, perhaps, a walk[29] is not absolutely forbidden, provided that one remains alone. Just as real flight is to be viewed as pernicious, so also is the unfortunate tendency to force one's misery upon others. The desert fathers were absolutely not opposed to human contact. Quite the contrary! We would not possess the numerous collections of their "Sayings," had they not spoken.

Contact with like-minded friends was also not in the least forbidden to the anchorite.[30] What was prohibited was the unfortunate tendency to "spiritual indiscretion," that embarrassing "talkativeness" which can keep for itself neither the manner of God's grace nor the attacks of the adversary.[31] Prohibited was every type of unhealthy

---

[25]*Apophthegm Arsenios* 11.
[26]*Pr* 58.
[27]See below, Ch. 6, "Acedia and the Spiritual Life."
[28]*Mn* 55.
[29]*Am* 35, 10.
[30]*R. m.* 7.
[31]*Ep* 16, 5.

familiarity (*parrhēsia*) which, like a scorching wind, burns real friendship and trust.

Much could be said about friendship among monks, even, and above all, among these desert inhabitants who were far less crude than we like to imagine. In his *Scholia on Proverbs*, Evagrius devoted moving passages to this "spiritual friendship," friendship in and through Christ, who himself is "our friendship." His *Letters* also bear testimony to the tactfulness with which he cultivated such friendships, whose cement is not only human (and therefore frequently fleeting) affection, but the "knowledge of Christ," which makes those who possess it into "friends of Christ," entirely like John the Baptist and the Apostles, whom Christ himself called "my friends."[32] As friends of the same person they become friends of one another, and even friends of the holy Angels. But let us return to our theme!

*

False familiarity (*parrhēsia*) was thus scorned, and so was "opening of the heart"; this was a uninersally obligatory praxis used on all sides, but was in any case reserved to the spiritual father alone. To him, in order to obtain his advice and his judgment, one was allowed to disclose, unreservedly, without false shame, one's secret struggles and defeats, and also one's victories and spiritual experiences. The text of Palladius quoted above shows how considerately Evagrius himself knew how to perform this delicate task. We have also seen that Evagrius, though he was a famous Abba, had such a close friend, in whom he confided and on whom he relied for advice and judgment.

These spiritual fathers, and mothers, were (and, in the Christian East, are) not at all exclusively priests, monks, or nuns. Evagrius himself remained a deacon all his life. Of the approximately 5,000 monks in the desert of Scetis, in whose neighborhood Evagrius lived in the company of 600 trained ascetics, only eight were priests.[33] The majority of the famous spiritual fathers of the desert must have been lay people, almost in the modern sense of the word, since monasticism did not yet have a fixed canonical status.

[32]Jn 15.14.
[33]*HL* 7.

Spiritual fatherhood or motherhood was indeed not tied to an office, but, on the contrary, was a *charisma*. It could not be decreed, but was conferred on one who in the achievements of his life attained such a depth of experience in all his defeats and victories as no "book learning" can bring about. This charisma is not tied to any age. Many of these "fathers" and "mothers" were quite young, even for conditions of the time. Macarius the Great, for example, was called the "young Elder" because of his youth.

Today, particularly in the West, one frequently laments that there are no more spiritual fathers, but one forgets that in the domain of grace it is not the father who makes the son, but, on the contrary, *the son makes the father*. What is missing in modern western human beings is the spirit of "filiation," from which all spiritual fatherhood comes into being.[34] A description of the spiritual father from the mouth of a famous contemporary Coptic desert father, Father Matta al-Maskin, teaches us why this is so. In a personal letter of the monks of the Macarius monastery it is said about their life that:

> The spiritual father is above all a human being who has allowed himself to be led by the Spirit and who has become a docile tool in God's hand. Therefore he will not attempt to call the disciple to be an imitator of him, for all of us are disciples of Christ, who himself is the sole master. Never will he stand at his side, escorting him, since he is but a human being and not an angel. Rather he follows him humbly, like a servant, in order to be helpful, when needed, to the one who, like himself driven by the Spirit, follows in the footsteps of Christ. This requires that he, even more attentively than the disciple himself, listen to what the Spirit of God wants for his spiritual son and he thereby entirely disregards what may appear to him as personally advisable. The disciple will hear from his mouth only the word of God, not mere human wisdom.

From such self-effacing service, one always knows how to distinguish a real spiritual father in the Christian sense from any type of self-styled "guru," of which sort of person there is truly no lack today.

[34]See G. Bunge, *Geistliche Vaterschaft*.

A real spiritual father will never found a "school." What outlives his own "spirit" is only that share of the Spirit of God, which was awarded to him. Let us remember what was said about the "transfer of the Spirit" from Antony the Great to Macarius of Egypt.[35] The perseverance of the anchorite in the seclusion of his cell reflects an extreme human situation, but its symbolic value is incalculable. Most people do not live in "cells" but in equally confined situations of all types, in the family, an occupation, and so forth. To persevere there in silence and without bitterness and resentment, but with one's gaze fixed rather on the "outcome," makes the human being into a monk (*monachos*) in the real sense of the word, which means that one is completely "unified."

On the other hand, a mere clenching of one's teeth would in the long run be an all too negative attitude, which ultimately would serve rather to fix the despondent person's gaze on his difficult situation than to free him from it. On the very spot where experience teaches that despondency is in the habit of breaking in with its dissolving effect, it is necessary to build a dam, a positive attitude, which protects one from falling.

In a few words—significantly at the end of the chapter on despondency—Evagrius outlines an entire strategy for driving away this vice. He gives indeed a little rule of life.

> Steadfastness,
>   and that one does everything with great care,
>   fear of God and perseverance, [these] heal
>   despondency.
>   Set for yourself

---

[35] *Historia Monachorum in Aegypto*, c. XXI, 2, in André-Jean Festugière, ed., *Historia Monachorum in Aegypto*: Édition critique du text grec et traduction annotée, Subsidia Hagiographica 53 (Brussels: Société des Bollandistes, 1971). — Abba Macarius of Egypt (or Abba Macarius the Egyptian), d. 390, the founder of the monastic settlement at Scetis, visited Antony the Great at least twice. Like Antony, Macarius was viewed as a "Spirit-bearer" (in Greek, *pneumatophoros*, indicative of "prophetic gifts"). For a discussion of Macarius, see Antoine Guillaumont, "Macaire l'Égyptien," in *Dictionnaire de spiritualité* 10 (1980): 11–13.—*Tr.*

> a goal in every task
> > and do not rise from it
> until you have finished it.
> > And pray unceasingly, and express yourself
> > concisely,
> and the spirit of despondency
> > will flee from you.[36]

"Set for yourself a goal in every task" is the basic rule, which Antony the Great, "first of the anchorites," had already learned from the mouth of an angel when he was oppressed by despondency. In the end, acedia is not a temptation to be immoderate, whether through negligence, or in a more opaque way through excess. Evagrius is certainly not a fanatic for rules:

> It is not always possible to follow the customary rule at all times; one should rather take the circumstances into consideration and attempt to the best of one's knowledge and powers to fulfill all precepts that can be fulfilled.[37]

Here, this "customary rule" is no written rule of the order; the monasticism of Scetis did not yet know such a thing. What is meant, rather, is a kind of measure that everyone, with the advice of the more experienced—and on the basis of the experience of one's own possibilities and limits—has to establish himself. Under normal conditions, it is a matter of following one's personal rules with unquestioning loyalty. In exceptional cases, one makes use of evangelical freedom. This delicate working-together (*synergia*) of obedience and freedom is typical of the spirituality of the ancient fathers. We will soon consider the reasons for this.

*

A proven means to prevent the restlessness of acedia, and to become its master once it has spread, is work. Hard but steady work, performed with care and moderation, which is neither an end in itself

---

[36] *O. sp.* 6, 17–18.
[37] *Pr* 40.

nor an occasion for disgraceful avarice—the monks have at all times
made this their duty. Evagrius gives the deeper reasons:

> Take care to work at manual labor, and, when possible, work by day
> and by night, in order not to be a burden on anyone. But also, above
> all, in order to be able to give [to others], as the Holy Apostle Paul
> reminds in exhortation.[38] Again, also to overpower the demon of
> despondency, and to remove other desires [that come] from the
> enemy. The demon of despondency pounces upon idleness, and
> every idle person is filled with covetousness, as it is said.[39]

Here, in a few lines, Evagrius condenses the spiritual experience
of the desert fathers, whose disciple and heir he is. Numerous texts
from the *Apophthegmata* could illustrate every sentence with a little
episode. At that time, when physical labor was still an affair of slaves,
the fathers valued working with their hands in an uncommon way;
they were equally conscious of the dangers of work degenerating into
covetousness and unhealthy activism.[40]

It really takes no less *self-discipline* to finish a work with diligence
than to let it lie there when other, more important obligations arise.
Benedict rightly instructs that nothing be preferred to the Office.[41]
At all times, it is a matter of putting an end both to idleness and to
becoming a "workaholic" and pursuing working for its own sake,
independent of anything else. Evagrius' fine gift of observation dis-
cerns forms of despondency in both extremes.

*

Courageous endurance, that is to say, the activation of the natural
functions of the soul's incensive part is, nevertheless, not the only
remedy against despondency. The soul's desiring power is likewise
attacked and alienated from its natural function. Evagrius defines
three specific virtues as follows:

[38]See 1 Thess 2.9; 2 Thess 3.8; Eph 4.28.
[39]*R. m.* 8; see Prov 13.4.
[40]See the sequence of the texts cited above, *R. m.* 8.
[41]Rule of St Benedict 43.

It is the task of level-headedness to look dispassionately at things which stimulate in us irrational images; the task of love consists in showing itself to every image of God almost as it does toward its prototype, even when the demons lay hands on it to defile it; it is the task of temperance to push away with joy any pleasure of the palate.[42]

One recognizes easily, or can guess, the various temptations of despondency that are directed against these three virtues of the desiring power of the soul. We have given numerous examples above: the irrational desire for things that are not available or cannot be realized, all kinds of impure feelings and irrational desires. It would lead us too far afield if we were to cite here all the pieces of advice Evagrius gives as remedies for the restoration of the natural function of the desiring part of the soul. It suffices to consider moderation a bit more closely.

The problems of obesity; of seeking "consolation" through joy in the delights of the palate; of the evil of over-eating, today so widespread yet scarcely understood in its essence; and many others, were not unknown to the ancients. On ethical grounds they used a remedy which is still practiced today for aesthetic or health reasons: fasting. Evagrius says laconically:

> The one who controls the stomach
> diminishes the passions;
> by contrast, the one who is defeated by food
> increases lusts.[43]

By fasting, the monastic fathers understood not only the complete or temporary renunciation of particular types of food, such as meat. They preferred the rule of Paul: *"Eat whatever [is sold] without raising questions of conscience."*[44] Even more important was the conscious *curtailing of needs,*[45] a renunciation of refined and expensive foods,[46] above all when we long for a variety of tasty meals.[47]

---

[42]*Pr* 89.
[43]*O. sp.* 1, 2.
[44]1 Cor 10.25ff; see *R. m.* 10.
[45]*R. m.* 3
[46]*R. m.* 8.
[47]*Pr* 16

At the same time, Evagrius is by no means a fanatical rigorist. The one who has to eat three times a day or even more frequently out of weakness or illness, instead of taking the single meal of the monks after 3:00 pm, should not trouble himself;[48] even less should one be disturbed if the sacred duty of hospitality, which perforce sets aside every "rule," requires that the fast be broken even several times a day.[49]

Nor, of course, does Evagrius approve of exaggerations in the opposite direction. Thus he advises a nun:

> Do not say: today I eat and tomorrow I do not eat!
> For you do not do this intelligently.
> This damages your body
> and it prepares stomach troubles for you.[50]

No matter how severe the asceticism of the desert fathers might be, it is always moderate, that is, appropriate to the strengths of each individual. It is never the inflexible performance of a legal coercion, but is always done under evangelical freedom, as Evagrius explains frequently. The justification of this freedom is founded in the fact that fasting, like other ascetical exercises, belongs to the "voluntary sacrifices" man brings to God spontaneously, without being held to it by a divine command.[51] For Evagrius sees the intrinsic meaning of all these exercises mainly in the *formation of the will*.

> Abstaining from foods, therefore, should be a matter of our free resolve and an effort of the soul.[52]

As a "voluntary sacrifice," fasting is adapted to the strengths of each.[53] The things we renounce are not unclean, for they were all created by God for our use, and God has not created anything evil.[54] The true cause of all evil lies in our "unclean hearts,"[55] in the perma-

[48]*R. m.* 10.
[49]*Loc. cit.*
[50]*Vg* 9.
[51]47 *in Ps* 118.108.
[52]*R. m.* 10.
[53]*Loc. cit.*
[54]2 *in Ps* 145.8.
[55]Mt 15.18.

nent misuse that we deliberately inflict upon God's creation.[56] The root of the primitive sin of the human being lies in this self-seeking distortion.

> The desire for food
> produced disobedience,
> and the delight of its taste
> expelled man from Paradise.[57]

Accordingly, it is understandable not only why gluttony (*gastrimargia*), which literally signifies "uninhibited stomach," is the first of the eight generic vices, but also why fasting, the renunciation of the elementary enjoyments of the palate, is the first virtue.

> The first of the [heathen] nations
> is Amalek.[58]
> And the first of the passions
> is gluttony.[59]
> The one who possessed a jawbone[60]
> destroyed those of a different race,
> and he tore up his chains
> with ease.[61]

*

All these worldly-wise recommendations and observations alone, however, will not accomplish much, because the desiring and incensive part of the soul have their roots in the *irrational*, instinctive domain, which by itself is not in a position to correct its faulty conduct. Ultimately, the impetus toward action must come "from above" if anything is to change in this befuddling complex of frustration and aggression. The stimulus to change can come only from the "intel-

---

[56]*KG* III, 59.

[57]*O. sp.* 1, 10.

[58]Num 24.20.

[59]*O. sp.* 1, 3.

[60]A reference to Samson, who besieged the "ones that are of a different race," a symbol of the demons. See Judg 15.14–16.

[61]*O. sp.* 1, 7.

lect," the seat of the image of God in man, and man's capacity for
God, which can be drawn out from the passions of the soul into compassion, and which does not lose its responsiveness to God's word.
The intellect remains the sanctuary of free decision, which imparts to
all human performance its worthiness or worthlessness.

In order to emerge from the dead end of despondency, it is essential to appeal to the intelligent power (*logistikon*), which has a governing function (*hēgemonikon*) in the human being.[62] Following his
master, Gregory of Nazianzus, Evagrius defines the working of the
rational part of the soul in accordance with nature and creation, in this
way:

> Since the rational soul, in accordance with our wise teacher, is tri-
> partite, virtue, when it is found in the mental part of our soul, is
> called prudence, sagacity, and wisdom . . .
>
> Now, it is the task of prudence to lead the campaign against hostile
> forces, to protect the virtues, to position the battle lines against vice;
> and in contrast, to manage neutral things appropriately in the cir-
> cumstances of the moment.
>
> It is the task of sagacity to administer harmoniously all that is ben-
> eficial to our goal; by contrast, that of wisdom is to contemplate the
> reasons for corporeal and incorporeal beings.[63]

One of the secrets of the spiritual life is this: do all "*at the proper
time and with moderation. For what is exorbitant and unseasonable is of
short duration. What is of short duration, is, however, rather harmful than
useful.*"[64] For one of the tasks of prudence is "to manage neutral things
appropriately in the circumstances of the moment." Evagrius eluci-
dates what is meant with the example of psalmody.

As we have seen, acedia produces a diffuse listlessness at
psalmody, which makes the recitation of the texts oppressive for us.
One is then tempted, if not to sleep during the entire office, then to
"do things at the wrong time," by which is meant drawing out the

---

[62]See *Pr Prol* [2]; *Or* 21.
[63]*Pr* 89.
[64]*Pr* 15.

psalms by singing them when they should be recited. Then again the
demon urges us to undue haste . . . " Prudence knows how to offer
resistance against this:

> From time to time, at the synaxis, one ought to whisper the psalm.
> From time to time, on the contrary, it is essential to continue with
> psalmody in the approved manner. According to the cunning of the
> opponent, we must change [our conduct].[65]

One should behave in a similar way when the demon attacks our
flesh and such tiredness comes over us that we are tempted to remain
lying in bed.

> If we awake from sleep before the synaxis, let us will to practice in
> our heart thoughts of the light, so that, well prepared and with a
> wakeful spirit, we may be in condition to stand ready for psalmody.[66]

As has already been said many times, the victory over despondency is linked to a promise, the deeper sense of which we still need
to fathom.

> The one who exercises the soul in advance, in order to be illumined
> by excellent thoughts, wipes the pillar of prayer shiny in anticipation
> . . . The one who continuously reflects the glow of prayer takes pris-
> oner the lowest thoughts through the highest contemplation, while
> his intelligible eye receives its power as nourishment from the light.
> The one who continuously gives himself over to contemplation of
> higher things will receive keen sight, as is reported about the prophet
> Elisha.[67]

What Evagrius here recommends to Eulogius the monk concerning the Office, the pre-eminent "work of God," applies naturally,
mutatis mutandis, to any task. He who gets up at the last minute may
be certain that he will begin his work sullenly and with full dislike.
The same holds for the task itself. The one who lets himself be
pressed to improper haste, or lets himself be lured to negligence,

[65] *Eul* 9.
[66] *Eul* 9.
[67] *Eul* 9.

becomes in the end a victim of despondency. In this case, as Evagrius says, one must always do the opposite of what the adversaries recommend to us,[68] and with great diligence bring to its completion every task begun. One must give oneself a proper push when one is making no more headway.

These are all quite basic pieces of wisdom for daily life, and they are familiar to everyone. But very few people are aware that such small things determine whether our life goes to ruin in an eternal monotony full of sulkiness and dislike, or whether our heart will be filled "with thoughts of light."

*

Basic life wisdom may prevent one from falling into despondency, but if one is already right in the middle of it, stronger remedies are required. Following the fathers, Evagrius mentions several, which to modern people at first seem rather strange. *Tears* are the first remedy and are frequently mentioned.

> Heavy is the sadness
> > and unbearable is the despondency.
> But tears to God on high
> > are more powerful than either.[69]

One can weep for very different reasons, and tears do not always have the same meaning. Although tears are only a means, one can distort them into an end in themselves, and so lose one's mind.[70] The tears of which Evagrius speaks here are most intimately linked to prayer. For the ancients, praying meant paradoxically also shedding tears before God at the same time.

> In the midst of tears,
> > call upon the Lord at night,
> and let no one be aware

---

[68] *Pr* 22.
[69] *Vg* 39.
[70] *Or* 7, 8.

that you are praying,
and you will find grace.[71]

When the intellect sees [the charge of the demons] let it take refuge
with the Lord [. . .] and [looking up to heaven] speak with tears:

"Lord Jesus, power of my salvation, incline your ear to me, make
haste to save me. Be for me a God of protection and a place of refuge
in order to deliver me."[72]

Use tears, in order to be successful with all your requests.

For your Master receives prayer with tears exceedingly gladly.[73]

What might be the reason for this high esteem of tears? Why is
God so well pleased with prayer that is offered with tears? The answer
is found in Holy Scripture. The tears of the woman who was a great
sinner,[74] the tears of Peter after his disgraceful denial of the Lord,[75]
express without words the declaration the publican in the Temple
made in the words of Psalm 50: "God, have mercy on me, a sinner."[76]
Mute tears are the admission of one's own need for deliverance.
Christ did not come to summon the just, who need no repentance,
but sinners who declare themselves as such. Therefore, when Evagrius, following the fathers, recommends tears so forcibly, namely at
the beginning of prayer, it is because he wants to lead one to the indispensable acknowledgement of one's sinfulness and one's need for salvation.

The beginning of salvation
is to condemn oneself.[77]

Not only do tears shed in prayer indeed exert an influence on
God, but they also and above all lead to a change in us.

[71]Vg 25.
[72]*M. c.* 34. In this "short prayer," Evagrius combines Ps 139.8 and Ps 30.3.
[73]*Or* 6.
[74]Lk 7.37ff.
[75]Mt 26.69ff.
[76]Lk 18.13.
[77]*Sent* 1.

Before all else, pray to receive [the gift] of tears, in order to soften through repentance the inherent hardness of your soul; and while confessing your ungodliness before the Lord against yourself, you will attain the remission of sins.[78]

Indeed, nothing hampers us so much when we receive God's grace as does obtuse "bestial" savagery (*agriotēs*). Tears therefore necessarily belong to the "practical" life, which means asceticism and its toil, after which the peace of the knowledge of God will follow.

Those who sow in tears will reap with joy.

Going out, they went with tears, carrying their seed; but coming back, they shall come with joy, carrying their sheaves.

Those who perform *praktikē* with toil and tears "sow with tears"; but those who receive knowledge without toil, "will harvest amid joys." Meanwhile, at his word, one should observe that all of us come into life possessing the seeds of virtue [and thereby become certainly capable of *praktikē*]. And just as tears are linked to the seeds, so is joy to the sheaves.[79]

The fruit of the seeds is the sheaves, that of the virtues is knowledge. And as the seeds are accompanied by tears, so are the sheaves by joy.[80]

Since this is so, and since Christ in the Beatitudes promised joy for those who weep,[81] it is understandable how Evagrius can say:

> The spirit of despondency
> drives away tears;
> the spirit of sadness
> thwarts prayer.[82]

Despondency is the most malicious enemy of tears and of prayer coming from the heart. Thus to soften this inner hardening and brutalization, nothing helps so much as to have recourse again to tears.

[78] *Or* 5.
[79] 3 *in Ps* 125.5–6.
[80] *Pr* 90.
[81] Lk 6.21.
[82] *Mn* 56.

*

But what to do when even urgent requests for the gift of tears do not have the desired result, while that "loss of spiritual sensitivity," of which Evagrius spoke earlier, has nested itself as an enduring condition? Prudence knows another well-tried means of salvation: *Antirrhēsis* or counter-statement against the persuasion of the enemy. This "method," to which Evagrius has devoted one of his most voluminous works, the *Antirrhētikos*, consists essentially of the repeated recitation of specific verses from Scripture with the aim of making the enemy shut his mouth. Of course, one must, as in every case, be on guard for possible misuse.

> Thus, when the fathers from Scetis contradicted evil thoughts, they possessed great simplicity and fear of God. However, for us this is no certain [method], for the evil one is not at a loss for words, and then, deprived of the dialogue with God, we are busy all day long conversing with the enemy.[83]

The wrong kind of "counter-statement," which degenerates into an endless altercation with the demon, can only be described as a caricature of what was originally intended. Great "simplicity of heart" and "fear of God" are necessary presuppositions. What is intended with this "method," used widely by the early monks, is taught by the example of Christ, to which Evagrius expressly refers. As Christ was tempted in the desert by the demon, he did not enter into an endless discussion with the adversary, who, in fact, "is not at a loss for words." Rather, he broke off each discussion, and he thereby stopped the tempter's mouth with a word of God.[84]

*

Being hard-pressed, at times one does not have the most suitable "answer" to the promptings of the demon at hand, so Evagrius has, in his *Antirrhētikos*, ordered a multitude of passages from Scripture and

[83]J. Muyldermans, *À travers la tradition manuscrite d'Évagre le Pontique* (Bibliothèque du MUSÉON 3), Louvain (1932) 89, n. 32.
[84]*Ant Prol.*

arranged them according to the eight generic "thoughts." In the chapter on despondency, from which we have already quoted frequently, tears are not lacking:

> On the hardened soul, which at night sheds no tears because of thoughts [provoked by] despondency: The shedding of tears is in fact a great remedy against nightmares which result from despondency. The prophet David administered this remedy in a prudent way to his passions, for he said:[85]

> > "I am weary with my moaning,
> > every night I flood my bed with tears,
> > I drench my couch with weeping."[86]

> On the soul that believes tears signify nothing at the time of the struggle with despondency, and does not remember David who did this, in that he said:[87]

> > "My tears have been my bread
> > by day and by night."[88]

* * *

Many of the passages presented by Evagrius are indeed short prayers, as Augustine called them when he heard of this practice of the Egyptian monks. From this simple principle the tradition of the Eastern Church later developed[89] the so-called "Jesus Prayer." Without laying emphasis on a particular situation, the confession of Jesus Christ as the one redeemer, the call for help and mercy, and the admission of one's own sinfulness are combined in a concise formulation.

The Coptic tradition, within whose environment the Jesus Prayer truly emerged,[90] traces it back to Macarius the Great, the teacher of

[85]Ps 6.7.
[86]*Ant* VI, 10.
[87]Ps 41.4.
[88]*Ant* VI, 19.
[89]See G. Bunge, *Geistgebet*, Ch. II, "Pray without ceasing."
[90]See A. Guillaumont, *"La prière de Jésus chez les moines coptes,"* *Aux origines du monachisme chrétien.* (*SO* 30), Bellefontaine (1979) 127–134 ; *id., "Une inscription copte sur la Prière de Jésus,"* *loc. cit.* 168–183.

Evagrius, and it counts Evagrius himself among the early transmit-
ters.[91] This tradition can hardly be a fabrication, as will be shown in
a moment, although it might be hard to identify the real "inventor"
of "one-word prayer." One finds the short invocation, "Jesus, Son of
David, have mercy on me!" already in the mouth of the blind Bartimaeus.[92]

We have seen that Evagrius recommends[93] an "uninterrupted,
prepared short prayer" against the temptation of acedia, and that this
prayer, which one should perform with tears, should be directed to
Christ.[94] In his writings, he speaks everywhere of "short, concise,
uninterrupted, incessant, intense . . . prayers." In the light of certain
demonic annoyances, he advises, for example,

> At the time of such temptations,
> Practice a short and intense prayer.[95]

Accordingly, this prayer will consist of only very *few* words, and
in itself it will indeed be multiform, but at the core there will always
be an extremely concise formula containing an invocation to the Son
of God, which the early monastic writings have preserved for us. Further, according to Antony the Great, the word "unceasingly" means
that the prayer should be repeated as frequently as possible and as
evenly as breath,[96] as the fathers taught from the words of 1 Thessa-
lonians 5.17.[97] Like the other fathers of this early time, Evagrius may
not have known a fixed "formula," but standardizing first on the personal level of the individual who prays, and finally among monks in
general it becomes a very natural process, which of course has not
abandoned an original freedom in choice of words, not even today.

[91]*Am* 160, 11ff.
[92]Lk 18.38. In Mt 20.31, we read: "Lord! Have pity on us, Son of David"; and in
Mk 10.47, "Son of David, Jesus, have pity on me." Essentially, the text deals with the
same "one-word prayer."
[93]*O. sp.* 6, 18.
[94]*M. c.* 34. In order to make of verse Ps 139.8 a "Jesus prayer," Evagrius replaced
the second "Lord," in the invocation "Lord, Lord," by the name of Christ!
[95]*Or* 98.
[96]See *VA* 91, 3 where Antony in the struggle with demons advised: "Have no fear,
but on the contrary *always breathe in Christ* and believe in him."
[97]See *Pr* 49.

Evagrius must therefore unquestionably be counted among the earliest masters of the "one-word prayer." The famous Abba Isaac taught John Cassian the "fiery prayer," which is reduced to one psalm verse: *Deus, in adiutorium meum intende; Domine, ad adiuvandum me festina.* "O God, come to my aid; O Lord, make haste to help me."[98] Cassian is probably repeating the teaching of Evagrius, whom he had come to know in Egypt. Next to Evagrius, Cassian is one of the oldest witnesses of this tradition, which ultimately goes back to Antony the Great.

*

The meaning of the "method" of counter-statement, which emerged as the fruit of an intensive meditation on Scripture by the ancient fathers, is easy to understand. In place of the promptings of the enemy it puts the consoling, warning, promising words of God, which enable a human being to overcome deadness at the core of his being. The words of God break, as it were, a vicious circle of thoughts—that endless inner reasoning, one's own or from external sources—which has driven many out of their wits. How one uses counter-statement in detail, Evagrius teaches in the two texts that follow, one of which the illustrator of the Carolingian Psalter of St Denis may have had before his eyes.

> When we are attacked by the demon of despondency, then, in tears, we divide the soul into two halves, one of which comforts and the other is comforted, in that we sow good hope for ourselves and we sing the enchanting words of David:[99]

> "Why are you filled with sadness, my soul? Why are you so distraught? Trust in God for I shall give praise to him. He is the one who saves me, the light of my eyes, and my God."[100]

Not by accident does Evagrius quote a psalm. The Psalter is indeed the book of Holy Scripture with which Christians in general,

---

[98]Ps 29.2. This prayer is also addressed to *Christ*!
[99]See Ps 41.6.
[100]*Pr* 27.

and not just monks, have been most familiar, from time immemorial, thanks to its use in daily prayer. Evagrius' teaching that a *healing effect* goes out from psalmody to the soul is undoubtedly based on this daily experience.

> While songs inspired by the demons incite our desire and plunge our soul into shameful fancies, the "psalms, and hymns, and spiritual songs"[101] invite the intellect to the constant memory of virtue by cooling off our boiling anger and by extinguishing our lusts.[102]

As is well known, acedia arises from the simultaneous and long-lasting excitement of both irrational parts of the soul. Psalmody is therefore an excellent remedy against despondency: it appeases our aggressiveness, as Evagrius repeatedly states.[103]

Singing psalms correctly is, of course, an art, even a charisma, for which a man must pray, as for all divine gifts of grace.[104] It is not sufficient "only to move the tongue in the mouth!" It is more important to psalmodize "from the heart,"[105] "intelligently and orderly."[106] "Intelligent psalm-singing"[107] signifies "to psalmodize without distraction," in so far as the intellect is not impressed by the manifold images of the psalms themselves, nor does it linger with them, or on the things signified by the psalms, that is, their sensory content.[108]

In itself, psalmody belongs to the domain of "the manifold wisdom of God"[109] as it is reflected in creation[110] and in salvation history. Now, since this manifold quality does not let our intellect come to rest, and in fact makes it more "*manifold*,"[111] "psalmodizing without distraction" is an even greater thing than "*praying without distrac-*

[101]Eph 5.19.
[102]*Pr* 71.
[103]*Pr* 15; *Mn* 98. See also *Or* 83.
[104]*Or* 87.
[105]*Vg* 35.
[106]*Or* 82.
[107]Ps 46.8.
[108]1 *in Ps* 137.1.
[109]Eph 3.10.
[110]*Or* 85.
[111]*Or* 58.

tion,"[112] though prayer itself is "*a prelude to the spiritual and simple knowledge*" of God himself.[113]

Naturally, the demons know all this very well, and they find ways and means to spoil healing psalmody, and turn it into its opposite!

> Sing us one of the songs of Sion:
>> Demons are also known to me, who force us to recite "*psalms and spiritual canticles*," in which is contained even the command, which we, having gone astray, have transgressed, so that, when they hear it, they may mock us as the sort who "*say and do not do*."[114] David therefore also says,[115] "the proud will not mock me!"[116]

We must not be taken in by such cunning, least of all when we are depressed by despondency; yet psalmody is an activity becoming the human being, just as singing hymns befits the angels.[117]

*

Wisdom, whose task is "to contemplate the reasons of corporeal and spiritual objects"[118] and thereby gain insight into the secret context of our created being, can in the end provide the victim of despondency with one further remedy, which to modern man, at first sight, does not appear to be very tempting: practice at dying, the renowned *melete thanatou*.

> Our holy and most experienced teacher [Macarius the Great] has said: the monk will be so prepared at all times as if he were to die tomorrow, and on the other hand, he should deal with his body as though he still has many years to live together with it. The first, he said, cuts off despondent thoughts, and makes the monk more zealous; the latter, on the contrary, keeps his body healthy and makes it always preserve an even temperance.[119]

[112]*Pr* 69.
[113] *Or* 85.
[114]Mt 23.3.
[115]Cited by Evagrius from memory, see Ps 24.2 and Ps 118.122.
[116]2 *in Ps* 136.3.
[117]97 *in Ps* 118.171.
[118]*Pr* 89.
[119]*Pr* 29.

What is meant by this "practice at dying" emerges clearly from the text. Having its secret roots in self-love, despondency is, if nothing else, the expression of an exaggerated and unhealthy valuation of earthly, material life and its inevitable vicissitudes and misfortunes. In the place of this, the "practice at dying" instructs us that we do not have our true homeland here. It teaches (us) to evaluate the realities of this life dispassionately and to live accordingly. The second half of the saying teaches us that this entirely conscious "living for the moment of death" is nevertheless carried out simultaneously with a thoroughly healthy will for life.

The deeply Christian meaning of "practice at dying" is expressed beautifully in the following text:[120]

> The completion of life consists of this practice unto death, for the will of God. It brings our intellect to unite itself with God. And indeed it is the same, to die for God through the power of hope, and to live in God, as it is written: "For as many of you as have been baptized into Christ, that is, into his death, have put on Christ,"[121] the one who in truth is the resurrection of the soul. And in the last days, through his power, all flesh will be restored to life, and will be completed in those who partake of him, and he will unite them with the Father, and in the consummation of his life to the praise of the glory of the Holy Trinity.[122]

The following text is to be understood in the same sense, though at first sight it may seem to have an unchristian prejudice, and one unfriendly to the body. Evagrius links traditional Greek wisdom to the Christian ethos and discloses the deep, symbolic meaning of the monastic *anachōrēsis* (withdrawal) and life in the desert. Each Christian, who is indeed destined to freedom in God, is called upon daily to die to "the old man" and to mortify its selfish lusts, to relinquish his

---

[120]This text is probably not by Evagrius, but must be ascribed to the *Chapter of the Students of Evagrius*. For the latter, see [Évagre le Pontique] *Chapitres des disciples d'Évagre. Editio princeps* of the Greek text, introduction, translation, notes, and index by Paul Géhin, (SC 514), Paris (2007).

[121]Gal 3.27.

[122]J. Muyldermans, "Évagre le Pontique: Les Capita cognoscitiva dans les versions syriaques et arméniennes," *Le Muséon* 47 (1934): 90.

"body of death"[123] and "to come home to the Lord,"[124] if he wants to remain true to his calling. The manifold forms of monastic "asceticism," of "practice" in the virtues, have no other meaning than to create room for this "coming home" and "dying unto life."

> To separate the body from the soul is the privilege only of the One who has joined them together. But to separate the soul from the body lies as well in the power of the one who pursues virtue. For our fathers gave to the "practice at dying" and "the flight from the body" a name: *anachōrēsis.*"[125]

"Withdrawing," that is, withdrawal from the inhabited, developed areas into uninhabited wasteland, which is referred to here, is indeed a "spiritual event," and the monastic withdrawal into the desert is its corporeal symbol.

> An anchorite is one who lives piously and uprightly in the cosmos that exists in the mind.[126]

*

Spiritual knowledge or wisdom will ultimately do more than is necessary: it will let us see the deeper coherence hidden behind the misery of despondency. Man will then no longer say: "There is no one who sees my distress," because he understands, with Job,[127] that "on the side of God, for him there is still an affliction."[128] He will realize that the Apostles too were tempted in the same way.[129] And when "the soul does not recognize that this also, to be tempted for the sake of the will of Christ, is a gift of the Spirit," then it will become apparent with the help of a word like Philippians 1.29: "*For he has bestowed on you the grace not only of believing in Christ but also of suffering for him.*"[130]

---

[123]Rom 7.24.
[124]2 Cor 5.8.
[125]*Pr 52.*
[126]*Sk 14.*
[127]Job 34.9
[128]*Ant VI, 34.*
[129]*Ant VI, 49; cf. 2 Cor 11.23–28.*
[130]*Ant VI, 51.*

The human being slowly realizes that these "temptations" are necessary; indeed that one cannot be saved without them.

> Just as an athlete cannot be crowned if he does not contend in the wrestling match, so too can no one become a Christian without a struggle.[131]

> The one who flees from beneficial temptation flees from eternal life,[132] for the one who does not endure torments for the sake of the Lord, will not see the bridal chamber of Christ.[133]

Despondency, the depression of the soul, over time loses its apparently quite senseless and simply destructive character, so that—and this is a paradox—it becomes a way of being a true Christian in the imitation of Christ.

> During his life on earth, he offered up prayers and entreaty, with loud cries and with tears, to the one who had the power to save him from death, and, winning a hearing by his reverence, he learnt obedience, Son though he was, through his sufferings, when he had been perfected, he became for all who obey him the source of eternal salvation.[134]

---

[131]*Inst. mon.* II, 17.

[132]J. Muyldermans, "Evagriana. Le Vatic. Barb. Graecus 515." *Le Muséon* 51 (1938) 202, n. 17.

[133]*Loc. cit.*, n. 18.

[134]Heb 5.7ff.

CHAPTER 6

Acedia and the Spiritual Life

A ll these remedies against despondency may appear to the reader as not particularly helpful since all amount, more or less, to a renunciation of any type of surrogate satisfaction. "Renunciation," many will object, "is that not the best way, in fact, to *intensify* this feeling of frustration and aggression?" Certainly it would be if renunciation were without a horizon, without *prospect*, without any hope at all of reaching beyond the mere cessation of the hopeless condition.

Acedia is experienced by those affected by some type of *dead point* in the spiritual life. One cannot imagine ever rising again from the abyss. However, in various texts of Evagrius, one is reminded that after the apparent standstill, the horizon does open again quite suddenly, and it widens. Evagrius refers openly to a very particular experience which we now want to investigate. His discourse is about *rest*.

> The spirit of despondency
> drives the monk from his cell,
> but the one who has endurance
> will always have rest.[1]

What type of rest is the text concerned with? Evagrius has already indicated that this most oppressing of all demons is not immediately followed by another one. On the contrary, after he has been driven out, what appears is "a state of deep peace and an ineffable joy."[2]

Furthermore, it is said that acedia endured patiently puts the soul to the test beyond all bounds and makes it "well tested to the highest

---

[1] *O. sp.* 6, 5.
[2] *Pr* 12.

degree."[3] For this purpose only does God allow this, that the human being, like Job, be subject to trial.

Examining and testing are technical expressions derived from metallurgy. Silver and gold are tested in the fire and are purified of all waste material. Similarly, the testing of acedia is said to purify the soul of the waste product of the passions and to make it "shiny."[4] The "pillar of prayer" of one so tested becomes "radiant."[5]

While despondency makes the soul "sick to the eyes with regard to contemplation," and thus robs it of its power of vision, the soul becomes "keen-sighted" when it resists and "receives its sustenance from the light"[6] of divine reality.

> If as a result of the strain, a certain despondency should befall us, then we will ascend a little on the "rock" of knowledge, and we will occupy ourselves with the Psalter,[7] plucking the strings of knowledge through the virtues. And then we will graze the "sheep" once more under Mount Sinai, so that "the God of our fathers" may call even to us out of the Burning Bush [as he called to Moses][8] and bless us[9] equally with "the powers of signs and miracles."[10]

Thus, there is infinitely more at stake than one may at first suspect! This rest, which "passionlessness" signifies,[11] is a state of deep peace and an ineffable joy, a luminous heart and a sharp-sighted eye of the mind: all these are key concepts of Evagrian mysticism. Therefore, we must ask ourselves what this unexpected reversal, which from every point of view assigns to acedia a special place, actually means.

The texts examined previously indicate in what direction we have to search: it is a question of the loftiest goal of the human being, the contemplation of things divine, namely those *insights of this age which*

[3] *Pr* 28.
[4] Mn 55.
[5] *Eul* 9.
[6] *Eul* 9.
[7] What is meant is the intellect.
[8] See Ex 3ff.
[9] *M.c.* 17.
[10] Ps 104.27
[11] *M.c.* 11.

the Lord gave to man, as a good shepherd to the sheep, so that he may graze *them*,[12] that is, he may be occupied with them.[13] The "*God of our Fathers*," mysteriously hidden in the burning bush, speaks to him directly, and in this very personal encounter reveals the true "reasons" for the "signs and miracles" which he has worked in creation and in salvation history, and which he is still working!

Let us feel our way cautiously into this inmost area of the mysticism of the monk from Pontus.

*

It is clear from several texts that there exists a characteristic and intimate link between acedia and prayer. To begin with, it is thoroughly negative:

> The spirit of despondency
>> drives away tears,
> the spirit of sadness
>> thwarts prayer.[14]

As we have seen, tears are indispensable for prayer that is pleasing to God. Accordingly, as acedia drives out these tears, it means that *the heart* is transposed to a state of "rawness" and spiritual "insensitivity," which the tears will, of course, dissolve.

> A despondent monk
>> is dilatory at prayer.
> And at times, he does not
>> speak the words of the prayer at all.[15]
> Despondency:
>> a dislike of prayer.[16]

What weight these sayings have in the mouth of Evagrius can be understood when one pays attention to the significance prayer has in

---

[12]*M.c.* 17.
[13]Eccl 3.11.
[14]*Mn* 56.
[15]*O. sp.* 6, 16.
[16]*Vit* 6.

his eyes. It is not only one human occupation among many, but the very action in which man is truly himself.

> Prayer prepares the intellect for this purpose:
> to carry out its own activity.[17]

Evagrius defines prayer exactly as a "prelude to immaterial and simple knowledge"[18] of God himself. Prayer is "a dialogue with God without any intermediary,"[19] whether a creature or even a very pure "thought" about creation. Clearly no created things are in themselves hindrances on the way to God. They are, on the contrary, "letters" which tell of their Creator. Only those who are "far from God"[20] stand in need of them. The goal is not to experience something about God, but to meet the Persons of the Holy Trinity directly.[21] Therefore, what Evagrius says becomes understandable:

> Prayer is that activity which is appropriate to the dignity of the intellect, that is, it is the intellect's pre-eminent and most authentic application.[22]

It is precisely here, in the direct encounter between image and archetype, that man's likeness to God comes to its full development, as far as this is at all possible on earth. But if this is so, then acedia brings man (if he remains stuck in it) to the most profound experience he can ever have in this life.

It follows that prayer is thus the best means to recognize one's inner condition,[23] for in prayer the bill for our life to date is presented.[24] This is true above all for the two components of despondency: frustration and aggressiveness, from which arise sorrow, grief, and anger.

---

[17] *Or* 83.
[18] *Or* 85.
[19] *Or* 3.
[20] *Ep.Mel.* 5ff.
[21] *Or* 60.
[22] *Or* 84.
[23] *Ep* 25, 6.
[24] *Or* 12.

Do not give yourself over to an angry thought so as to fight in your mind with the one who has offended you; nor again to a thought of fornication, in that you imagine uninterrupted lust. The first darkens the soul; the other invites you to the fire of the passions, but both cause the intellect to be defiled; and while at prayer time you imagine these [corresponding] images, and thus do not offer pure prayer to God, you fall prey to the demon of acedia. He falls with predilection upon souls in this [spiritual] condition, and tears the soul to pieces as a hunting-dog does a fawn.[25]

Accordingly, Evagrius insistently urges *reconciliation* with one's opponent, even before one makes ready for prayer.[26] Otherwise all effort is in vain.[27] Great prudence and discernment are needed before one ventures to bring the incense of one's prayer to the "intelligible altar" of God,[28] and woe to the one who, though he remains impure and full of passion—above all of anger—audaciously risks mimicking[29] prayer that requires reverence "in spirit and in truth!"

Above all it is the sins of anger with which we are confronted in prayer.[30] Only the one who is free of anger is able to pray serenely![31] But anger arises frequently from frustrated desires.

When you are armed against anger, you will never tolerate a desire. The latter indeed gives anger its subject matter and anger then clouds the intelligible eye of the intellect and so blights the state of prayer.[32]

Acedia and prayer mutually exclude each other. Despondency is a deadly poison that constantly watches for even the most advanced mystic so as to rob him of his "enlightenment."

[25] *Pr* 23.
[26] *Or* 21.
[27] *Or* 22.
[28] *Or* 147.
[29] *Or* 146.
[30] *Or* 24.
[31] *Or* 26.
[32] *Or* 27.

On the intellect that does not understand that the thoughts of acedia, when they endure in him, upset his condition and at the time of
prayer darken the holy light in his eyes . . . [33]

As the rest of the text teaches, neither Evagrius nor his friend
Ammonios were at that time fully aware of where that mysterious
light originated: is the intellect itself light, or is it illumined by a light
that is found outside it?

Like acedia, sadness[34] also—and naturally anger[35]—darken this
"holy light." Here, the question is not of some experience of sense-
perception, for what is meant by this "light" is rather knowledge or
contemplation, as Evagrius draws from Scripture:[36] "kindle in us a
light of knowledge."[37]

My heart is bewildered . . . and the light of my eyes is not with me:

The "light of the eyes" signifies contemplation, which retreats from
the intellect at the time of temptation.[38]

Then, the intellect itself is "light," illuminating, and under well-
defined preconditions it is able to "see" this.

It is evidence of passionlessness that the intellect has begun to perceive its own gleam of light.[39]

Again, no sensory perceptible experience is meant. Rather, at this
moment, the intellect becomes like a "knowing substance"[40] of its
own nature, which was created only for this [purpose], to *know God*.[41]
Likewise, the reverse follows:

As the cloud prevents the rays of the sun from shining, so does anger
extinguish the soul's gleam of light.[42]

---

[33] *Ant* VI, 16.
[34] *Ant* IV, 61.
[35] *Ep* 28, 1.
[36] See Hos 10.12.
[37] 4 *in Ps* 33.6 and in other places.
[38] 6 *in Ps* 37.11.
[39] *Pr* 64. See Gen 45.
[40] *KG* I, 3.
[41] *KG* I, 89.
[42] *Inst. mon.* II, 2.

Dulled anger, it is said at another place,[43] "blindfolds" the [spiritual] eyesight [of the intellect]. In other words, the "darkening" of the intellect signifies that it becomes unable to fulfill its natural function of "being the light of the mind,"[44] that is, of "knowledge."[45] For Evagrius, "knowing" always means "seeing,"[46] and *vice versa*. Indeed, like the body, the intellect has "eyes,"[47] and to be sure, a left and a right eye, which carry out their own functions.

> Demonic thoughts blind the soul's left eye, which is devoted to the contemplation of creation; by contrast, thoughts that imprint and shape our intellect, blur the right eye, which at the time of prayer beholds the blessed light of the Holy Trinity. It is through this eye also that the Bride in the Song of Songs delighted the heart of the Bridegroom himself.[48]

*

The intellect itself is *light*, a "light" and as such it is able to experience itself, in that it beholds its "own light." But this light is received as a gift, since the intellect, according to its nature, is a "lamp,"[49] destined "to take up into itself the divine light"[50] and thereby knowingly to "perceive." With both its "eyes," the intellect beholds God indirectly in creation through its sensory contents (*logoi*) and also *directly*. This direct-personal encounter is the event which Evagrius calls "prayer" in its most profound, mystical sense: a shining out of the divine glory. *Prayer is an intellectual state that comes into being only through the light of the Holy Trinity.*[51]

Naturally, we do not intend any process perceptible to the senses,[52] but the *experience of the revelation of the Person of God in the*

---

[43]*KG* V, 27.
[44]*Or* 75.
[45]*KG* I, 74.
[46]17 *in Ps* 69.29.
[47]*KG* II, 35.
[48]*M.c* 42. See *HL* 4, 9.
[49]See Mt 6.22.
[50]16 *in Ps* 17.29.
[51]*Sk* 27.
[52]See the warnings in *Or* 13 and *Ant* VII, 31.

person of man. For if the intellect is freed from the passions that darken it[53] and the light of its eyes is unclouded, in the state of prayer it becomes fully aware not only of itself, "the beauty of its creaturely likeness to God," which then shines on it as "Light"[54] (for according to 1 Jn 1.5, God in his essence is "Light"),[55] but it contemplates in this light also the radiant Light-and-Glory of the Holy Trinity, with which it is clothed,[56] and and with which it is intermingled,[57] with the result that one can no longer distinguish between these two "Lights."[58] For according to its natural purpose as a creature, the intellect is a "dwelling-place of God":[59] a "place" of the personal presence of the radiant splendor of the triune God. Only one who has experienced this is able to speak of it.[60]

> Just as it is not the same to see the light and speak of the light, so is it not the same to see God and to understand something about God.[61]

This state of mystical "enlightenment" is what Evagrius means most profoundly by "knowledge" (*gnōsis*). Here "prayer," "contemplation" (*theōria*), and "knowledge of God" are one. For what is meant is that condition of the most perfect and intimate oneness which is possible only between persons who "know" one another. Accordingly also, the union between Christ and his Father is the "model" of the life of grace for us, the *eschaton* (last thing) of the promised union between God and creation,[62] which the one who prays already experiences "in the state of prayer."[63]

[53] *KG* V, 15.
[54] *Cent Suppl* 50.
[55] *KG* I, 35.
[56] *Cent Suppl* 53.
[57] *KG* II, 29.
[58] *Ant* VI, 16.
[59] *Sk* 34.
[60] *Or* 67.
[61] *KG* V, 26.
[62] Jn 17.21. See G. Bunge, "Mysterium Unitatis. Der Gedanke der Einheit von Schöpfer und Geschöpf in der evagrianischen Mystik," *Freiburger Zeitschrift für Philosophie und Theologie* 36 (1989), 449–469.
[63] See G. Bunge, *Geistgebet*, Ch. V, "Der Zustand des Gebetes."

*

Now if acedia, or rather its accomplices, sadness and anger, disturb this condition, then it is understandable why Evagrius declares categorically:

> Prayer is the elimination of sorrow and dejection.[64]

But to this negative definition of prayer is contrasted a positive one:

> Prayer is a fruit of joy and thanksgiving.[65]

> When your mind, because of an intense longing for God, divests itself a little, so to speak, of the flesh, and turns away from all thoughts that proceed from sensory perception, or from memory or temperament, while it is at the same time filled with fear of God and joy, then you may assume that you are near the boundaries of prayer.[66]

It is very significant that Evagrius does not simply identify prayer and joy. Prayer is not just a state of joy! It is rather a fruit of joy and still lies beyond these boundaries, as we shall see more clearly later. This distinction is not unimportant because it keeps us from considering feelings of happiness and things like that already as the goal, or still worse, to speculate about similar feelings. That is, as in the case of tears,[67] to distort the means by making it into the end.

> When, standing at prayer, you attain no other joy, then you have truly found prayer.[68]

Acedia is the exact reverse of joy. The one who "endures" during temptation "will always pray with joy."[69] Indeed an "ineffable joy,"[70] unknown until that point, falls within his reach, a joy that lies "beyond

[64] *Or* 16.
[65] *Or* 15.
[66] *Or* 62.
[67] *Or* 7, 8.
[68] *Or* 153.
[69] *Or* 23.
[70] *Pr* 12.

any other joy." It is this fullness of the "joy" which only Christ can give.[71] It follows mourning at the departure of Christ,[72] and no one is able to take it away from believers.[73]

Hence, this much is certain: prayer in the sense intended by Evagrius is possible only when a deep, spiritual pacification and conciliation have occurred, far from all bewilderment by the passions, and beyond all over-excitement and emotionality. It is very significant that Evagrius, unlike so many spiritual authors, does not use the concept of ecstasy in a positive sense. It always signifies a negative state of being outside oneself.[74] Prayer is a state of perfect rest and clarity of the intellect. This prudent attitude of Evagrius, which continues to stand out clearly, is one of the most satisfactory and trustworthy signs of the authenticity of his spiritual teaching, indeed of his entire mysticism.

*

What is true for joy holds to an even greater extent for *peace*, the "peaceful state" of which it is said that it follows the attack of acedia, provided that we endure.[75] However, here Evagrius makes an important distinction at once, which can also hold true for joy.

> There are two peaceful states of the soul: the first grows from natural seeds, the second arises from the retreat of the demons. Now on the first state follows humility, along with compunction, tears, a boundless longing for what is godly, and a measureless zeal for work. In the case of the second, vainglory along with arrogance brings about the monk's downfall through the disappearance of the other demons. Now whoever watches over the boundaries of the first state, will quickly recognize the incursions of the demons.[76]

The distinction is clear: the first form of peace grows out of the natural soil of our being, in that God, at our creation, sowed the inde-

[71]Jn 15.11.
[72]Jn 16.20.
[73]Jn 16.22.
[74]*Pr* 34.
[75]*Pr* 12.
[76]*Pr* 57.

structible seeds of the Good.[77] Only Christ gives this peace,[78] he also *is* this very peace, as Evagrius, with Paul,[79] keenly observes.[80]

The second peaceful "state" is entirely different: it is nothing other than an illusion, a skillful diversionary maneuver of the demons, which will suggest thoughts to the monk, that this withdrawal is the result of his *own* ascetical exertion.[81] The one who lets himself be deluded has to expect a concentrated attack by his opponents.[82]

*

With the chapter of the *Praktikos* quoted above, Evagrius opens a series of descriptions of "the state where impassibility is near." The condition that Evagrius describes here is the one he describes elsewhere as an "imperfect impassibility."[83] Perfect impassibility, which the soul acquires after a victory over all the demons, is defined by Evagrius in the following manner:

> "Fullness of peace" is the impassibility of the soul, together with a real knowledge of things in themselves.[84]

> Passionlessness is a peaceful state of the rational soul; it results from meekness and prudence.[85]

This state of inner silence is the natural condition of the intellect,[86] that is, its created being as willed by God, which is troubled only secondarily by the various passions. In the same manner, it is by nature proper to the intellect to be light.[87] Both images assert one and the same thing—and this indeed is the heart of the matter: The intel-

---

[77] *KG* I, 39, 40.
[78] 2 *in Ps* 84.9.
[79] Eph 2.14.
[80] 1 *in Ps* 71.1.
[81] *Ant* VIII, 4, 6, 13, *et passim*.
[82] *Pr* 44.
[83] *Pr* 60.
[84] 11 *in Ps* 36.11.
[85] *Sk* 3.
[86] See *Or* 70.
[87] See *Pr* 64.

lect is designed to have a capacity for God, and its likeness to God lies in this capacity.[88]

For Evagrius, passions, sins, are always something "alien" that is forced upon us from outside, something that expresses itself in the "darkness" and "confusion" of the intellect. On this basis, one also recognizes, incidentally, the drawing near of an angel, in whom God comes near to us indirectly, but unmistakably, in the deep peace that he spreads in the soul. The approach of the demon, on other other hand, is known by uneasiness, anxiety, confusion, and so forth,[89] which he provokes in the soul, even if, in order to delude [the intellect], he has disguised himself as an angel of light.[90]

*

From what has been said, it is clear what Evagrius means by "a state of deep peace" and "ineffable joy" that follow upon the victory over despondency: there are indications that with God's help[91] the human being has overpowered the remaining passions and now sets foot in the domain of passionlessness, the necessary condition and direct boundary of "the place of prayer,"[92] or "place of God,"[93] that is, the contemplation of the Holy Trinity. What an unforeseen perspective!

Let us pursue this thought a little more. A series of texts develops ideas which have already been touched upon, into a mysticism of the "indwelling of God" in the blessed soul.

> From holy David we have learned clearly and distinctly what the "place of God" is. He says: "His place is established in peace,[94] and his dwelling in Sion."[95] Consequently, the rational soul is "the place of God," but his "abode" is the luminous intellect, which has

---

[88]*KG* VI, 73.
[89]*Ant* VIII, 17; *Or* 75; *Pr* 80.
[90]*Ant* VIII, 24.
[91]*Pr* 33.
[92]*Or* 57.
[93]*Or* 58.
[94]This is how the LXX translates the Hebrew *Salem*; see also Heb 7.2.
[95]Ps 75.3.

renounced worldly pleasures and is instructed to investigate the symbolic principles of the earth.[96]

This "luminous" (*phōtoeidēs*) intellect is the one that first beheld its "own gleam of light" and was then adorned "by the light of the Holy Trinity" so that one can no longer distinguish between the two "lights." In the following chapter, Evagrius mentions the prerequisites for this mystical sight.

> The intellect is not able to see "the place of God" in itself, if it has not been successful at rising above all thoughts of [perceptible] things; and it cannot rise above them when it does not divest itself of the passions that shackle it through the thoughts of such sensory things. Now, it will divest itself of the passions by the virtues, and of the ordinary (mere) thoughts by spiritual contemplation and this, again, if that light shines on it, which at the time of prayer marks "the place of God."[97]

It is easy to understand that the passions prevent us from seeing *in ourselves* the "place of God" because they defile the intellect, and "*wisdom* never enters a soul meditating on evil, nor does it dwell in a body devoted to sin."[98] Now, since "our God is wisdom,"[99] "real wisdom,"[100] it goes without saying that "wisdom will rest only in a good heart."[101] But why do we have to divest ourselves of the "simple" (*psiloi*), pure, image-free knowledge containing thoughts of the things of creation? Because they are an intermediary between us and God,[102] but we are destined to hold "dialogue with God, without any intermediary at all."[103]

---

[96] *Sk* 25.
[97] *M.c.* 40.
[98] Wis 1.4.
[99] 5 *in Ps* 131.7.
[100] *Ep.fid.* 6, 2.
[101] Prov 14.33.
[102] *Or* 54–58.
[103] *Or* 3.

When the intellect has put off "the old man" and put on the [new] man, born of grace,[104] then at the time of prayer it will behold its own condition as resembling the color of sapphire or of heaven. In Scripture, this same condition is called "the place of God," which the elders beheld on Mount Sinai.[105]

Here Evagrius refers to the mysterious appearance of God to Moses and the elders of the people of Israel at Mount Sinai.[106] At the same time (according to the LXX), they beheld "the place where the feet of the God of Israel stood. And what was beneath his feet was like a work of sapphire flagstones and, as it were, the view of the *firmament of heaven* in its purity."[107]

Then again, the thought is quite obviously not about a somehow sense-perceptible, even colorful, manifestation, since "only" metaphors are involved. The "new man," who is born in baptism, obtains his true being at the time of prayer in his perfect, created, and now renewed[108] inner purity and grace, and experiences himself as the "place" of the personal presence of God, who has "taken up his abode in him."[109] But even this highest mystical experience of God always remains threatened in this life.

[Scripture] also calls this place a "vision of peace,"[110] in which one sees in oneself that peace which surpasses all understanding and which guards our hearts.[111] For in a pure heart, another heaven is engraved, whose vision is light and whose place is spiritual, in which, in a certain sense, the ideas of things which exist are perceived. Moreover, the holy angels frequent those who are worthy. This vision, however, makes resentment appear dull; while the seething of anger through wrath disappears altogether.[112]

[104]See Eph 4.22ff; Col 3.9ff.
[105]*M.c.* 39.
[106]See Ex 24.
[107]Ex 24.10.
[108]Col 3.10.
[109]See Jn 14.23
[110]See Ps 75.3; Sk 25.
[111]See Phil 4.7.
[112]*Ep* 39, 5.

This beholding of the light and glory of God in the clear "mirror" of one's own self, cleansed of all darkening passions, which is the highest form of the knowledge of God that is possible in this life, will find its fulfillment in that "face-to-face" vision when "God will be all in all."[113]

> Only the Father . . . is both the End and also the final Blessedness. That is to say, when we recognize God no longer in a mirror and in external things,[114] but approach him as the One and Unique, at that point we will also recognize the final end.[115]

As the craving for this recognition is infinite[116] and leads to an insatiable desire for God,[117] so the knowledge of God itself is "without boundaries,"[118] an eternal growing and increasing in knowledge and love, indeed faced with the immensity of God in pure not-knowing.[119] Blessed is the one who has arrived at this insurmountable not-knowing.[120]

> A deified intellect is an intellect that from all agitation has arrived at peace and has been adorned with the light of the vision of the Holy Trinity and begs of the Father the fulfillment of a desire that is insatiable.[121]

*

What follows this ordeal of acedia, which challenges the human being in his deepest roots, when it is bravely endured, is therefore not merely a feeling of relief and satisfaction. With that, indeed, the human being remained only on the level of the psychic. That sudden and complete change signifies rather the *breakthrough to true personhood in the encounter with the Person of God.*

[113] 1 Cor 15.28.
[114] See 1 Cor 13.12.
[115] *Ep.fid.* 7, 18–22.
[116] *KG* IV, 50; *Pr* 57.
[117] *Or* 118.
[118] 5 *in Ps* 70.14; 3 *in Ps* 138.7.
[119] *KG* I, 71; III, 63.
[120] *KG* III, 88.
[121] *Cent Suppl* 53; see *KG* I, 65.

It is indeed God himself who entirely unexpectedly and of his own free will calls the human being out of the burning thorn bush of his seclusion, to bless him, too, as at one time he blessed Moses and Aaron[122] with an understanding of "the reasons for signs and wonders,"[123] not only the ones he once performed in Egypt, but also of those at first incomprehensible and dreadful things that happened to him.

What is more, he is the one who, in the very soul, the "place" of his mysterious indwelling, suddenly reveals his presence as radiant light and thereby at the same time makes visible the characteristic beauty of this soul, which was created "in his image and likeness." And he it is who now makes himself known as "Father," as the personal ground-of-being (*Urgrund*) of the Holy Trinity and, by grace, of all being.[124] He himself is this "peace," whom the blessed one now experiences, and who lets an "ineffable joy" break forth in him.

Viewed this way, acedia and the spiritual life belong inseparably together. In acedia, the *"old man, who is corrupted by deceitful lusts,"* ends up in a completely shattered state.[125] But this one, when he is destroyed, will be a "holocaust for God."[126] Only then can "the new man created in justice and holiness, after God,"[127] in that "first" or "little resurrection," rise to what is called the "spiritual life," a life entirely in the spirit of the Triune God.

[122]14 *in Ps* 104.27.
[123]*M.c.* 17.
[124]*Ep.Mel.* 25.
[125]Eph 4.22.
[126]*Ep* 61, 3.
[127]Eph 4.24.

Epilogue

O ur excursions through the writings of Evagrius have ostensibly carried us far away from our starting point, into unknown and unfamiliar regions. But this impression is only superficially correct. Despondency, as Evagrius understands and presents it, is an extremely complex and contradictory phenomenon, a *parting of the ways (Scheideweg)*, as it were. The one who reaches this point, depending on how he behaves, sets his foot either on a path that leads him sooner or later to a spiritual and sometimes even physical death, or on a path to life. Depression can mean the end or the beginning of true life.

*

Acedia is a vice, a *passion*, from which man *suffers* in the truest sense of the word, as from all passions or diseases of the soul. And, like all passions, it has its secret, invisible roots in self-love (*philautia*), that all-hating passion, which manifests itself in a thousand ways as a state of being stuck in oneself that renders one incapable of love. Its secret driving forces are anger, aggressiveness, and that irrational desire which distorts all creation in a selfish way. Because it is unnatural, this wayward desire cannot, in its essence, find fulfillment.

> You cannot possibly satisfy desire! For just as in those who have given themselves over to anger, bitterness [gall] arises [in ever new ways] on every occasion, and such people always increase these ways through the nourishment they take; so too do those who have surrendered to desire likewise increase their overpowering desire, whether they take nourishment or they contemplate the features of the body.[1]

---

[1] J. Muyldermans, "Évagre le Pontique: Les *capita cognoscitiva* dans les versions syriaques et arméniennes," *Le Muséon* 47 (1934): 101, n. 14.

Insatiable desire cannot be satisfied because it is directed at mundane things, which cannot satisfy us because they are limited. Created things do not have a meaning in themselves; their *logos* (reason) points beyond to the one to whom they owe their existence.[2] Whoever wants to seek them for other reasons will remain eternally frustrated. Such a desire is also insatiable because it goes against the proper destiny of the human being. "Thou hast created us for Thee, O Lord, and our heart is restless until it rests in thee."[3]

Therefore, with these insatiable *earthly* desires, Evagrius contrasts any desire which is directed at God, the desire for whom, he says, is also insatiable,[4] though this insatiability is of a different nature. It is founded not on the limitedness of that which is desired, which cannot correspond to the limitlessness of the desire of the one who desires, but rather on the illimitability of that which is desired.

> There is a longing (*pothos*) that is good and eternal, the one that strives for true knowledge; and, as is said, it cannot be separated from the intellect.[5]

The object of this "true knowledge" is *God*, but there is no object "that lies at the root of *our* knowledge,"[6] because he, and he alone, is "substantial knowledge."[7] With him alone being, or essence (*ousia*), and knowledge are one thing. In contrast to creatures, "God has no qualities"[8] that can be added to his Being. As limited creatures we are therefore not able ever to "embrace"[9] his Being, but we must let ourselves be "embraced" by him. Here, in a paradoxical manner, *knowing* becomes *not-knowing*.

---

[2] *7 in Ps* 29.8.
[3] St Augustine, *Confessions* I, I
[4] *Cent Suppl* 53.
[5] *KG* IV, 50.
[6] *KG* IV, 87; V, 62.
[7] *KG* I, 89; II, 47, 77, etc.
[8] *Ep.fid.* 3, 3ff.
[9] *Ep.fid.* 2, 37ff.

The one whose knowledge is limited, his not-knowing is limited as well. Therefore the one whose not-knowing is boundless, his knowledge is still limited.[10]

Our own limitedness limits also our knowledge of God, of whom it is said, "Of his greatness there is no end."[11] For this reason, therefore, "only the knowledge of the Holy Trinity is without limit, for it is intrinsic wisdom,"[12] and "blessed is he who arrives at this inexpressible not-knowing."[13] This "blessedness," indeed, will be bestowed on us in abundance only at the "end," precisely when the prayer of Jesus has been wholly fulfilled: "Father, grant that they, too, may be one in us, just as you and I are one."[14] "For as God is *one*, he will make all one when he has entered into each one, and number vanishes through the appearance of the state of Unity."[15]

In the [condition] of oneness [between God and the created intellect] an ineffable peace reigns, and now there are only mere intellects that at all times are satiated by the insatiableness [of this peace].[16]

*

The one who surrenders to fleeting desires deprives himself of the possibility of attaining in this life the foretaste of unending blessedness. Worse still, the frustration of our diffuse desires and the impossibility of their being fulfilled immediately call *sadness* onto the scene, the feeling of disappointment and emptiness, a condition that immediately precedes acedia. Fundamentally any arbitrary "thought" can become an incentive for despondency insomuch as all "thoughts" are linked to a fleshly desire. Sadness and acedia are then so intimately related to each other, without being identical, that Evagrius frequently mentions them in one breath.

[10]*KG* III, 63.
[11]*KG* I, 71 (citation Ps 144.3).
[12]2 *in Ps* 144.3.
[13]*KG* III, 88.
[14]Jn 17.21.
[15]*Ep.fid.* 7, 51–56.
[16]See *KG* I, 65.

Meanwhile, what characterizes acedia and makes it stand out from sadness is the simultaneous and long-lasting excitement of both irrational powers of the soul, the desiring and the incensive powers. Acedia delineates itself by the complexity of frustrated covetousness and aggression.

Despondency has, so to speak, a Janus head that, dissatisfied with the present and greedy for what is to come, is able to turn backwards and forwards. From this conflicting inner contradiction arise the partly paradoxical and totally extreme manifestations of lethargy and restlessness. As melting-pot and end-point of almost all the other "thoughts," and through its long duration, acedia eventually assumes all the forms of spiritual depression, which in the worst case can end in suicide, to avoid the last hopeless putting to the test.

*

Since the characteristic manifestation of evil is an inclination to flight in all conceivable forms, the specific remedies which Evagrius prescribes are reduced basically to one: sheer *persevering*! In this standing fast, the general healing of this diseased root of self-love is accomplished. To persevere also means to resist the urge of the irrational desires. Maximus the Confessor, who (as is well known) frequently let himself be inspired by Evagrius and his students in his *Four Centuries on Charity*, cites very appropriately in this context the word of Christ in Lk 21.19:

"By standing firm, you will save yourselves."[17]

This waiting is not a blind suffering, but a conscious *waiting for God*. There is only one way out of the vicious circle of acedia—when the human being breaks through the prison walls of his "I," of his hopeless isolation, and reaches real personhood, a transparency towards the other, and thereby also true love, finding himself in the surrender to the other's "You." But the human being can find his own personhood only in an encounter with the Person of God, in whom he him-

[17]Maximus Confessor, *Capita de Charitate*, I, 67 (PG 90:973D), see Lk 21:19. [In English, St Maximus the Confessor, *The Ascetic Life. The Four Centuries on Charity*, Polycarp Sherwood, tr. (NY: Newman Press, 1955) Ancient Christian Writers n. 21].

self is secured and hidden (as is all being). Since God himself is love, in the end only an encounter with him heals the fundamental evil of self-love, the plaintive expression of the anxiety of losing oneself in the surrender of the self.

*

As with endurance, other, subordinate remedies similarly aim at a direct personal encounter with God. Evagrius deliberately describes the tears that soften inner hardening and "brutalization" as "tears to God on high." The human being does not weep for himself alone or, for instance, out of sheer compassion for himself. He weeps before God, in that he admits his hard-heartedness towards him in the hope of being freed from it by God's mercy. In this turning away from his false "I," he becomes like the prodigal son on the way to his father, who then meets him, not in the father's house, but beyond expectation, while he is still on the way.

*

Again, the meaning of *antirrhēsis* ("counter-statement"), to be used against all seductive insinuations, is nothing else but the breaking of the ring of brass of one's own inner reasoning by the word of God, and arriving at a liberating *dialogue with God* instead of endless monologue.

As Evagrius explains in the prologue to his *Antirrhētikos*, the great example is Christ himself who, in the desert, did not allow himself to be caught by the false image of the Messiah that the seducer suggested with subtle arguments, but proved his true identity through resorting to the word of God.

*

In the end, for the Christian, the "practice at death" signifies nothing but a bringing to mind of the unavoidable moment when he will meet his Lord. For everyone will appear before the face of God whether they have waited for him ardently or have tried to avoid him all their lives. This practice unto death signifies a true qualification of earthly life, because it places everything in relation to God and thereby protects one from locking oneself up selfishly in one'a own self.

While acedia, in its consequences, is basically a "suffocating"[18] of the human person under the burden of the isolated "I," it is understandable how the overcoming of this condition can be experienced as a rapid lightning-like breakthrough to full personhood. In place of deadly desperation and helpless unrest, suddenly a deep peace and ineffable joy arise. They are the foretaste of what Christ promised his disciples on the eve of his Passion[19] and gave them in full reality as the Risen One on Easter morning.[20]

*

Peace and joy, not as the world pretends to give them, but as only the One who is "our Peace"[21] can bestow them; these are, as it were, the last step in the meeting of the infinitely small human being with the infinitely great God. Through it, the mortal being, already on earth, sets foot in the mysterious "place" Evagrius indicates as prayer, contemplation, knowledge of God, or theology, which here are all one.

For Evagrius, prayer is at its most profound an unending intimate dialogue between the human person and the Person of God, "without any intermediary,"[22] an expression of the limitless love of God as our Father,[23] who himself is the "first-love."[24] In other words, friendship with God, perfect and spiritual love,[25] will never cease growing.[26]

*

For a person of prayer, what Evagrius says in the closing chapter of his treatise *On Prayer* is essential:

> If when praying no other joy can attract you, then truly you have found prayer.[27]

[18]*Pr* 36.
[19]Jn 14.27; 16.20.
[20]Jn 20.12ff.
[21]Eph 2.14.
[22]*Or* 3.
[23]*Or* 54.
[24]*Ep* 44, 2; 56, 3.
[25]*Or* 77.
[26]*Or* 118.
[27]*Or* 153. [*The Philokalia. The Complete Text*, vol. 2, G. E. H. Palmer, Philip Sher-

In the "perfect and spiritual love" of the true "theologian"[28] the neighbor is also included. How could it be otherwise, for God himself proves his own "first-love" by this: "that he loved us first"[29] and "sent his Son as Savior of the world."[30] And "*by this we have known the love [of the Father], because his [Son] laid down his life for us.*"[31]

And thus, love for the brother becomes the *touchstone* of the authenticity of the love for God.[32]

> Blessed is the monk who regards everyone as God after God.[33]

> Blessed is the monk who with unmixed joy looks at everyone's salvation and progress as if they were his own.[34]

Such "monks" in the original meaning of the concept "*monachos*" (alone), wholly and absolutely "unified," are found everywhere, not only in the desert. They have transcended themselves, their false "I," which is nothing but the prison of their "all-hating self-love," and have found themselves and everything and all in God. Such a monk is indeed no longer "of this world," but he is no less "a stranger to the world." For in truth, he is closer to the world and his brethren than he is to himself.

> "A monk is one who is separated from all and united harmoniously to all."[35]

> "A monk is he who regards himself as existing with all men and sees himself in each man."[36]

From these heights of the mystical life, "a life hidden with Christ in God,"[37] acedia is, in a paradoxical way, always only one step removed.

rard, and Kallistos Ware, tr. (London: Faber & Faber, 1979), 71].

[28] *Or* 61.
[29] 1 Jn 4.19.
[30] 1 Jn 4.14.
[31] 1 Jn 3.16.
[32] 1 Jn *passim*.
[33] *Or* 121. [English trans. from *The Philokalia*; see above, n. 26].
[34] *Or* 122.
[35] *Or* 124.
[36] *Or* 125.
[37] Col 3.3.

But how difficult it is to take this small step! No one can be compelled to take it. How many, unfortunately, take the opposite step, which leads to death instead of to life, either the violent one or the slow, daily one through diversions and vain distractions. They deprive themselves of the one important experience it is necessary to have in this life. It would perhaps have been enough to persevere in silence only another short while.

> Come, my people, enter thou into thy chambers, and shut thy doors about thee; hide thyself as it were for a little moment, until the indignation be past. For behold! The Lord comes out of his place . . . [38]

*

This step beyond oneself everyone takes personally and yet not alone, for innumerable people have taken it before. The experience he has is indeed first of all that of the "Night" or of "Nothingness," as Isaac of Nineveh and John of the Cross and many others have described it. But even in this night, the unexpected light that is not of this world then shines for him. And then, when the poor, defeated, little man like Antony, the father of monks, amazed and reproachful, asks:

> "Lord, where were you then all the time, why did you not appear at once to relieve my affliction?"

he hears that strange, mysterious answer:

> "I was there nevertheless, Antony! But I waited in order to see your struggle."[39]

So greatly does God love and respect his creation that he leaves room for it in himself, so that this last small step may be taken towards God.

---

[38] Is 26.20ff.
[39] *VA* 10.

Works by Evagrius

[English titles following titles in other languages are provided for information only, and do not refer to actual pblished translations unless they are introduced by the words, "In English"].

ABBREVIATIONS:

CSCO   Corpus Scriptorum Christianorum Orientalium, Paris-Louvain, 1903ff.

GCS   Die griechischen christlichen Schriftsteller, Leipzig, 1897ff.

LNPF   A Select Library of Nicene and Post-Nicene Fathers of the Christian Church ed. P Schaff-H. Wace; rpt. Grand Rapids, 1951ff.

LThK   Lexikon für Theologie und Kirche, Freiburg i. Br., 1995.

OCP   Orientalia Christiana Periodica, Rome, 1935ff.

PG   Patrologia Graeca, ed. Jacques-Paul Migne, Paris, 1857–1866.

PO   Patrologia Orientalis, ed. R. Graffin and F. Nau, Paris, 1903ff.

SC   Sources Chrétiennes, Paris, 1941ff.

SO   Symbolae Osloenses, Oslo, 1920ff.

ST   Studi e Testi. Pubblicazioni della Biblioteca Vaticana, Rome, 1900ff.

TU   Texte und Untersuchungen zur Geschichte der altchristlichen Literatur, Leipzig, Berlin, 1882ff.

Ant   *Antirrhētikos* (*Talking Back*) ed. by W. Frankenberg, *Euagrius Ponticus*, Berlin (1912): 472–545. Italian trans. by G. Bunge, V. Lazzeri, *Evagrio Pontico, Contro i pensieri malvagi. Anti-*

rrhetikos. Bose (2005). [In English, *Talking Back: A Monastic Handbook for Combating Demons,* trans. by David Brakke, Cistercian Publications; Collegeville, MN, Liturgical Press, 2009].

Cent Suppl   Pseudo-Supplement to the *Kephalaia Gnostica (Gnostic Chapters),* ed. by Frankenberg, loc.cit.

Ep   *Epistulae (Letters)* LXII, ed. Frankenberg, loc. cit. German trans. by G. Bunge, Evagrios Pontikos. *Briefe aus der Wüste,* Trier (1986). Greek fragments in C. Guillaumont, "Fragments grecs inédits d'Évagre le Pontique," TU 133 (1987), 209–221. P. Géhin, "Nouveaux fragments des lettres d'Évagre," *Revue d'Histoire des Textes* 24 (1984): 117–147.

Ep. fid.   *Epistula fidei (Letter on the Faith).* Italian trans. and edit. by J. Gribomont, in M. Forlin-Patrucco, Basilio di Cesarea, *Le Lettere,* Vol. I, Turin (1983) 84–113. German trans.: G. Bunge, *Briefe,* 284–302. [In English, R. J. Deferrari, trans., *Saint Basil. The Letters.* Loeb Classical Library, vol. 1, Cambridge, MA (1926): 47–93].

Ep. Mel.   *Epistula ad Melaniam (Letter to Melania),* ed. by Frankenberg, loc. cit.; Part I; G. Vitestam, *Seconde partie du traité, qui passe sous le nom de «La grande lettre d'Evagre le Pontique à Mélanie l'Ancienne»* Lund (1964). [In English, M. Parmentier, trans., "*Evagrius of Pontus. Letter to Melania,*" in *Bijdragen, tijdschrift voor filosofie en theologie* 46 (1985): 2–38; trans. reprinted in *Forms of Devotion: Conversion, Worship, Spirituality, and Asceticism,* ed. by Everett Ferguson, NY: Garland (1999): 272–309]. German trans. by G. Bunge, *Briefe,* 303–328.

Eul   Tractatus ad Eulogium Monachum (*Treatise to Eulogius the Monk*), PG 79:1093D-1140A. We follow the text and the numbering of the edition of the better Greek text of the Lavra MS G 93 (E). [In English, *Evagrius of Pontus. The Greek Ascetic Corpus,* ed. and trans. by R. E. Sinkewicz, on the basis of the Greek text of the ms Lavra G 93 (E), Oxford Early Christian Studies, Oxford University Press, (2003): 310–333].

Gn   *Gnostikos (The Gnostic),* ed. and trans. by A. and C. Guillaumont, *Évagre le Pontique. Le gnostique ou À celui qui est devenu digne de la science.* SC 356, Paris (1989).

In Eccl   *Scholia in Ecclesiasten (Scholia on Ecclesiastes),* ed. and trans. by

P. Géhin, *Evagre le Pontique, Scholies à l'Ecclésiaste.* SC 397, Paris (1993).

In Prov *Scholia in Proverbia* (*Scholia on Proverbs*), ed. and trans. by P. Géhin , *Évagre le Pontique,* SC 340, Paris (1987).

In Ps *Scholia in Psalmos* (*Scholia on Psalms*). With the kind permission of M.J. Rondeau, who is preparing a critical edition of this work, on the basis of the MS *Vaticanus Graecus* 754, the collation of which we are using. See also, *id,* "Le commentaire sur les Psaumes d'Évagre le Pontique," in OCP 26 (1960): 307‒348.

Inst. Mon. *Institutio ad Monachos* (*To the Monks*), PG 79:1236–1240. *Suppl.* ed. J. Muyldermans, *Evagriana, Le Muséon* 51, Louvain (1938): 198ff.

KG *Kephalaia Gnostika* (*The Gnostic Chapters*), ed. and trans. by A. Guillaumont, *Les six Centuries des "Képhalaia Gnostica d'Évagre le Pontique,"* PO 28, Paris (1958). Greek fragments ed. by J. Muyldermans, *Evagriana.* Extrait de la revue *Le Muséon ,* vol. XLIV, augmented by "*Nouveaux fragments grecs inédits,*" Paris (1931); *id.* "*À travers la tradition manuscrite d'Évagre le Pontique,*" in *Bibliothèque du Muséon* 3 (1932); I. Hausherr, "Nouveaux fragments grecs d'Évagre le Pontique," OCP 5 (1939): 229‒233; Ch. Furrer-Pilliod, *Horoi kai Hypographai. Coll. Alphabétiques de définitions profanes et sacrées,* in ST 395 (2000). [In English, there is a translation of six centuries by David Brundy, in *Ascetic Behavior in Greco-Roman Antiquity,* ed. by Vincent Wimbush, Minneapolis: Fortress Press (1990): 175‒186].

M.c. *De diversis malignis cogitationibus* (*On Various Evil Thoughts*), ed. and trans. by P. Géhin, C. Guillaumont and A. Guillaumont, *Évagre le Pontique, Sur les Pensées,* SC 438, Paris (1998). [In English, *Evagrius of Pontus: The Greek Ascetic Corpus,* trans. by Robert E. Sinkewicz, *Oxford Early Christian Studies,* NY: Oxford University Press (2003): 136–182. See also, the *Philokalia: The Complete Text,* trans. by G.E.H. Palmer, Philip Sherrard, and Kallistos Ware; London: Faber & Faber (1971): I, 38‒52]. A partial English trans. may be found on pp. 117‒124 of *Early Fathers from the Philokalia,* by E. Kadloubovsky and G.E.H. Palmer, London; Faber & Faber (1978)].

Mn *Sententiae ad monachos* (*Sentences for Monks*), ed. by Hugo Gressmann, *Nonnenspiegel und Mönchsspiegel des Evagrios Pon-*

tikos TU 39, 3 (1913) 143–165. [In English, see *Evagrius Ponti-cus, Ad Monachos*, trans. by Jeremy Driscoll, *Ancient Christian Writers* 59, NY: Paulist Press (2003). See also *The Mind's Long Journey to the Holy Trinity: The Ad Monachos of Evagrius Ponti-cus*, trans. by the same, Collegeville, MN, Liturgical Press (1993)].

Or   *De oratione tractatus* (*Treatise on Prayer*), PG 79:1165A-1200C. J. M. Suarez, S.P. N. Nili Abbatis, *Tractatus seu Opuscula*, Rome (1673), 475–511; the treatise *De Oratione* (*PG* 79: 1165–1200C), and *Philokalia*, vol. I, Athens (1957), 176ff. German trans. *Philokalie der heiligen Väter der Nüchternheit*, vol. I, Würzburg (2004) 287–309. [In English, *The Praktikos. Chapters on Prayer*, trans. by John E. Bamberger, Cistercian Studies; Number Four; Cistercian Publications, Spencer, Massachusetts (1970). Another trans. may be found on pp. 54–71 of *The Philokalia, The Complete Text* compiled by St Nikodimos of the Holy Mountain and St Makarios of Corinth, and trans. by G.E.H. Palmer, Philip Sherrard, and Kallistos Ware. London, Faber & Faber (1970)].

O. sp.   *Tractatus de octo spiritibus malitiae* (*On the Eight Spirits of Evil*), PG 79:1145A-1164D. German trans. by G. Bunge, *Evagrios Pontikos. Über die acht Gedanken*, Würzburg (1992). Beuron (2, 2007). We follow the numbering by R. E. Sinkewicz, who took over our numbering and corrected it. [In English, *Evagrius of Pontus: The Greek Ascetic Corpus*, trans. by Robert E. Sinkewicz, *Oxford Early Christian Studies*, NY; Oxford University Press (2003): 66–90].

Pr   *Capita Practica ad Anatolium* (*Practical Chapters to Anatolius*), ed. and trans. by A. and C. Guillaumont, *Évagre le Pontique, Traité Pratique ou Le moine*, SC 170–171, Paris (1971). German trans. with spiritual commentary: G. Bunge, Evagrios Pon-tikos, *Praktikos oder der Mönch*, Cologne (1989), Beuron (2, 2008).[For an English trans. please see above, s.v. *Or*].

R.m.   *Rerum monachalium rationes* (*Reasons for Things Monastic*), *PG* 40: 1252–1264.

Sent.   *Sexti Pythagorici, Clitarchi, Evagrii Pontici Sententiae* (*Sentences of Sextus Pythagoricus, Clitarchus, and Evagrius Ponticus*), ed. by A. Elter, Leipzig (1892).

Sk   *Skemmata* (*Reflections*), ed. by J. Muyldermans, *Evagriana*, in

Le Muséon 44, augmented with "Nouveaux fragments grecs inédits," Paris (1931): 38ff. [In English, "The Sapphire Light of the Mind: the *Skemmata* of Evagrius Ponticus," trans. by William Harmless and Raymond R. Fitzgerald, in *Theological Studies* 62 (2001): 498–529].

Vg   *Sententiae ad Virgines* (*Statements to the Virgins*), ed. by Hugo Gressmann, op. cit. [English trans. by Sinkewicz, *op. cit.*, 131–135].

Vit   *De vitiis quae opposita sunt virtutibus* (*On the Vices that are Opposed to the Virtues*), PG 79: 1140ff. We follow the Sinkewicz numbering, pp. 60–65. See also *Textverbesserungen* (Text corrections), *loc. cit.*, 293–294.

OTHER SOURCE TEXTS

Am   E. Amélineau, *Histoire des monastères de la Basse Égypte*, Annales du Musée Guimet 25, Paris (1894).

Conl   *Johannes Cassianus, Conlationes*, ed. and trans. by E. Pichery, *Jean Cassien, Conférences*. SC 42, Paris (1955), SC 54 (1958), SC 64 (1959). [In English, *John Cassian, Conferences*, trans. by Colm Luibheid, NY: Paulist Press (1985) and *John Cassian. The Conferences*, trans. by B. Ramsey, NY: Paulist Press (1997)].

Disc   [*Évagre le Pontique*], *Chapitres des disciples d'Évagre*, ed. and trans. by P. Géhin, Paris, SC 514 (2007).

HL   *Palladios, Historia Lausiaca*, ed. by C. Butler, *The Lausiac History of Palladius*, Cambridge (1898) and (1904). [For a more recent trans. see Robert T. Meyer, *Palladius; The Lausiac History*, Westminster, MD, Newman Press (1965). German trans. J. Laager, *Palladius, Historia Lausiaca, Zürich* (1987).

HL [Syr]   *Id. Syriac version*, ed. and trans. by R. Draguet, *Les formes syriaques de la matière de l'Histoire Lausiaque* (CSCO 389/390 and 398/399), Louvain (1979).

HE   Socrates von Konstantinopel, *Kirchengeschichte*, ed. by G.C. Hansen (GCS); trans. by Périchon and Maraval, SC 477, Paris (2004), SC 493 (2005), SC 505 (2006) and SC 506 (2007). [In English, *Socrates of Constantinople*, trans. by A.C. Zenos,

LNPF, series 2, vol. 2 (1890): 1–178; reprt. Grand Rapids, MI (1952)].

HE   Sozomen Church History, trans. by C.D. Hartranft, LNPF, series 2, vol. 2 (1889): 236–427. Greek text ed. by G.C.Hansen; German trans. by G.C.S. Hansen, Fontes Christiani 73, 1–4, Turnhout (2004).

HM   Rufinus, Historia Monachorum in Aegypto, ed. by E. Schulz-Flügel, Tyrannius Rufinus. Historia Monachorum, sive De Vita sanctorum patrum. Patristische Texte und Untersuchungen 34, Berlin-NY (1990). [In English, The Lives of the Desert Fathers: the "Hisroria monachorum in Aegypto," trans. by Norman Russell, London: Mowbray and Kalamazoo; Cistercian Publications (1981).

VA   Vita Antonii, Athanasios of Alexandria. French ed. and trans., G. J. M. Bartelink, Vie d'Antoine (SC 400), Paris (1994). In English, The Life of Anthony, trans. by Robert C. Gregg, San Francisco: Harper (2006)].

Vita   Palladios, Vita Evagrii coptice, introduction, trans. and commentary by G. Bunge and A. de Vogüé, Quatre ermites égyptiens d'après les fragments coptes de l'Histoire Lausiaque (SO 60), Bellefontaine (1994): 153–175.

FURTHER EVAGRIANA BY THE AUTHOR

"Évagre le Pontique et les deux Macaire," Irénikon 56 (1983): 215–227; 323–360.
Evagrios Pontikos. Briefe aus der Wüste 24 (Sophia). Trier, 1986.
"Origenismus-Gnostizismus. Zum geistesgeschichtlichen Standort des Evagrios Pontikos," Vigiliae Christianae 40 (1986): 24–54.
"The 'Spiritual Prayer': On the Trinitarian Mysticism of Evagrius of Pontus," Monastic Studies 17 (1986): 191–208.
Das Geistgebet. Studien zum Traktat De Oratione des Evagrios Pontikos. Koinonia-Oriens XXV. Köln, 1987.
Geistliche Vaterschaft. Christliche Gnosis bei Evagrios Pontikos. Regensburg, 1988.
"'Priez sans cesse.' Aux origines de la prière hésychaste," Studia Monastica 30 (1988): 7–16.
Evagrios Pontikos. Praktikos oder Der Mönch. Hundert Kapitel über das geistliche Leben. Koinonia-Oriens XXXII. Köln, 1989; Beuron, 2008.

"Hénade ou Monade? Au sujet de deux notions centrales de la terminologie évagrienne." *Le Muséon* 101 (1989): 69–91.

"Mysterium Unitatis. Der Gedanke der Einheit von Schöpfer und Geschöpf in der evagrianischen Mystik." *Freiburger Zeitschrift für Philosophie und Theologie* 36 (1989): 449–469.

"'Nach dem Intellect leben.' Zum sog. 'Intellectualismus' der evagrianischen Spiritualität," "Simandron—Der Wachklopfer." *Gedenkschrift für Klaus Gamber*, ed. by W. Nyssen. Köln, 1989: pp. 95–109.

"Palladiana, I. Introduction aux fragments coptes de l'Histoire Lausiaque," *Studia Monastica* 32 (1990): 79–129 (81ff: "Évagre et ses amis dans 'l'Histoire Lausiaque'").

With Adalbert de Vogüé: "Palladiana III. La version copte de 'l'Histoire Lausiaque.'" II. "La Vie d'Évagre," *Studia Monastica* 33 (1991): 7–21.

These studies have been published as a book: G. Bunge and A. de Vogüé, *Quatre ermites Égyptiens d'après les fragments coptes de l'Histoire Lausiaque*. Spiritualité Orientale 69. Bellefontaine, 1994.

Evagrios Pontikos. *Über die acht Gedanken*. Würzburg, 1992; Beuron, 2007.

"Der mystische Sinn der Schrift. Anlässlich der Veröffentlichung der Scholien zum Ecclesiasten des Evagrios Pontikos." *Studia Monastica* 36 (1994): 135–146.

"Evagrio Pontikos, hl.," in LThK, 3 Auflage, Bd. 3 (1995), col. 1027–1028.

Evagrios Pontico. *Lettere dal deserto*. Introduction and Notes by Gabriel Bunge. Translation from the Greek and the Syriac by Salvatore Di Meglio and Gabriel Bunge. Magnano, 1995.

"Praktikē, Physikē und Theologikē als Stufen der Erkenntnis bei Evagrios Pontikos." *Ab Oriente et Occidente. Gedenkschrift für Wilhelm Nyssen*, ed. by M. Schneider and W. Berschin. St Otillien (1996): 59–72.

"'Créé pour être.' À propos d'une citation scripturaire inaperçue dans le 'Peri Archōn' d'Origène (III, 5, 6)." *Bulletin de littérature ecclésiastique* 98 (1997): 21–29.

"Evagrios Pontikos: Der Prolog des Antirrhetikos." *Studia Monastica* 39 (1997): 77–105.

Drachenwein und Engelsbrot. Die Lehre des Evagrios Pontikos von Zorn und Sanftmut. Würzburg, 1999. [In English, *Dragon's Wine and Angel's Bread, the Teaching of Evagrius Ponticus on Anger and Meekness*, trans. by Anthony P. Gythiel. St Vladimir's Seminary Press, 2009.]

"Erschaffen und erneuert nach dem Bilde Gottes. Zu den biblisch-theologischen und sakramentalen Grundlagen der evangrianischen Mystik." *Homo Medietas. Festschrift Alois Maria Haas*. Bern, 1999: 27–41.

"Aktive und kontemplative Weise des Betens im Traktat. *De Oratione* des Evagrios Pontikos." *Studia Monastica* 41 (1999): 211–227.

" 'La Montagne intelligible.' De la contemplation indirecte à la connaissance immédiate de Dieu dans le traité *De oratione* d'Évagre le Pontique." *Studia Monastica* 42 (2000): 7–26.

"La Gnosis Christou di Evagrio Pontico." In *L'Epistula Fidei di Evagrio Pontico*. Temi, contesti, sviluppi. Atti del III Convegno del Gruppo Italiano di Ricerca su "Origene e la Tradizione Alessandrina" (16–19 Settembre, 1998). *Studia Ephemeridis Augustinianum* 72 (2000): 153–181.

Evagrio Pontico. *Contro i pensieri malvagi*. Antirrhetikos. Introduzione di Gabriel Bunge. Traduzione di Valerio Lazzeri. Magnano, 2005.

"L'Esprit compatissant. L'Esprit, Maître de la 'prière véritable' dans la spiritualité d'Évagre le Pontique." *Buisson Ardent* 13 (2007): 106–123.

"In Geist und Wahrheit," Studien zu den 153 Kapiteln *Über das Gebet* des Evagrios Pontikos," *Hereditas* 27 (Bonn, 2010).

Names and Topics

Aaron 132

Abba Arsenius 92, 93

Abba Isaac 110

Abba Moses 92

Ab Oriente et Occidente 147

Acedia 18, 21, 23, 25, 36, 37, 45, 46, 48, 49, 54, 57, 58, 64, 69, 77, 79, 83, 85, 90, 92, 97, 111, 117, 118, 121, 125, 131, 132, 133, 136; A. a disease typical only of monks? 21–36; at the root of A. lies a frustrated desire 54; A. represents some type of dead end 57; consequences of A. on the life of prayer 77; Remedies of A. 87–115; A. not a harmless matter 90; A. a dead point in the spiritual life 117; A. and the spiritual life 117–132; link between A. and prayer 119

Acedia as a Janus figure 58, 136

Adam's love of self 62

Albinus 16

Amalek 101

Amelineau E. 145

Ammonios 132

Anachōrēsis 49, 114

Anchorite(s) 15, 19, 21, 23, 34, 47, 48, 68, 70, 79, 82, 84, 93, 97

Angel(s) 81, 94, 97, 130

Angel of light 128

Anger "blindfolds" the spiritual eyesight 123

Anger 43, 52, 54, 57, 62, 121, 123; in prayer, we are confronted with the sins of A. 121; sadness and A. darken the "Holy Light" 122; A. extinguishes the soul's gleam of light 122, 129

Angst, twin sister of acedia 48

Antirrhētikos 70, 73, 107, 137, 141

Antony the Great 11, 18, 34, 73, 96, 97, 109, 110, 140

Apatheia 40, 59, 63, 127; A. defined 59

Apophthegmata 73, 98

Archetype *(Urbild)* 120

Arians 13

Arrogance 52, 54

Asceticism 45; the severe A. of the Fathers always moderate 98

Athanasius of Alexandria 46, 146

Bamberger John E. 144

Baptism 33

Bartelink G. J. M. 146

Bartimaeus 109

Basil of Caesarea 13, 142

Baudelaire C. 25.

Bershin W. 147

Biography of Evagrius 12

Blasphemy 51, 52, 58

Brakke David 142

Bride in the Song of Songs 123

Briefe aus der Wüste 142

Brundy David 143

Bulletin de littérature ecclésiastique 147

Buisson ardent 148

Bunge Gabriel 11, 12, 16, 28, 55, 63, 77, 108, 124, 141, 142, 144, 146, 147, 166

Burning Bush 118, 119

Butler C. 17, 69, 145

Cain 48

Capita Practica ad Anatolium 144

Cenobites 15, 19, 34

Chapitres des disciples d'Évagre 145

Chastity 88

Chorepiscopus 12

Christ 24, 34, 38, 40, 41, 44, 87, 94, 95, 105, 106, 107, 109, 110, 115, 124, 126, 137, 138

Christliche Gnosis bei Evagrios Pontikos 146

Church 34

Church History 146

Clitarchus 144

Concept of philosophy 17

Conlationes 145

Constantinople 14

Contemplation of things divine 124

Contra i pensieri malvagi 148

Coptic monasticism 95

Coptic tradition 108

Cowardice 89

Created things are "letters" 120

Dam: building a D. against acedia 96

Darkening of the intellect 59

David 16, 109, 110, 113, 128

De diversis malignis cogitationibus 143

De octo vitiosis cogitationibus 22

De oratione tractatus 144

De Vogüé Adalbert 147

Deferrari R.J. 142

Deified intellect 131

Demon(s) 24, 25, 26, 27, 31, 32, 35, 37, 38, 39, 46, 55, 56, 63, 70, 79, 80, 81, 83, 84, 87, 91, 110, 112, 126; the D. not evil by nature 26–27; the D. a friend of exaggeration 79

Depersonalization *(Entpersönlichung)* 29

Der mystische Sinn der Schrift 147

Desert 24; D. the place where Christ overcame evil first and fundamentally 34

Desert Father(s) 11, 26, 31, 32, 33, 35, 48, 68, 73, 93, 94, 98, 100

Despondency 18, 46, 52, 53, 57, 60, 65–67, 69, 71–75, 77, 80–84, 87, 89, 90, 93, 97–99, 104, 106, 108, 110, 112, 114, 117–119, 121, 133, 136; D. manifestations of 65–85; D. disguises its true nature 80; Remedies for D. 87–113; D. a form of cowardice 90

De vitiis quae opposita sunt virtutibus 145

Di Meglio Salvatore 147

Dialectic 56

Discernment of Spirits 74

Discretion 15

Disintegration of the human personality 60

Drachenwein und Engelsbrot 147

Draguet R. 145

Driscoll Jeremy 144

Dwelling place of God 124

Education of Evagrius 13

Egyptian desert 14, 17

Egyptian monasteries 22

Egyptian monasticism 14

Egyptian monks 77, 108

Eight Thoughts: Gluttony, Lust, Avarice, Sadness, Anger, Acedia, Vainglory, and Pride 41

Eight Virtues: Temperance, Prudence, Poverty, Joy, Forbearance, Patience, Moderation, and Meekness 41

Elisha the Prophet 103

Elter A. 144

Endurance 92, 98

Epistula ad Melaniam 142

Epistula fidei 13, 142

Epistulae 142

Epistula LXII 142

Eulogius 103

Evagrii Pontici Sententiae 144

Evagrius 10, 11, 12, 14, 16–18, 21–23, 26, 32, 33, 38–46, 48, 52, 56, 62, 63, 65–69, 71–74, 79–81, 83–85, 87–89, 91–94, 96–100, 102–107, 109–111, 113, 115, 117–119, 121, 123, 126, 127, 130, 134, 135, 137, 138, 141–144, 146–148

Evagrius as calligrapher 16

Evagrius' sense of psychology 17, 53
Evil 26–30, 32, 33, 35, 37, 43, 62, 65, 68, 72, 80, 81, 87, 89, 100, 136; E. exists only as a parasite 27; personalizing of E. 27; E. definition of 26ff.; no E. can come from nature 26; e. is essential nothingness 44, 87
Excessive familiarity *(parrhēsia)* 94

False "I" 137, 139
Fasting 99
Father of Monks 21
Fathers of the Desert 94
Fear of God 88, 107
Ferguson Everett 142
Festugière André-Jean 96
Filiation, the spirit of 95; F. the son makes the father 95
Firmament of Heaven 130
Fitzgerald Raymond 145
Flowers of Evil 26
Forlin Patrucco M. 142
Formation of the will 100
Four Centuries on Charity 136
Frankenberg W. 141
Freiburger Zeitschrift 147
Free will 39, 62
Furrer-Pilliod C. 143

Gedenkschrift für Klaus Gamber 55, 147
Gehin P. 113, 142, 143, 145
Gift of tears 106, 107
Gihon 35
Gleam of light 129
Gnosis 30, 124
Gnostic 63
Gnostikos 45, 142
Good seed 81
Goodness of creation 44
Grace of baptism 31
Gregg Robert 146
Gregory of Nazianzus 12, 13, 17, 58–60, 102
Gresmann Hugo 143
Gribomont J. 142
Grief 72, 119

Guardini Romano 47, 48, 60
Guillaumont A. 12, 15, 17, 21, 96, 108, 142–144
Guillaumont C. 142–144
Gythiel Anthony P. 147

Hansen G.C. 145, 146
Harmless William 145
Harmony of wills 45
Hartranft C.D. 146
Hausherr Irénée 62, 143
Heart 31, 34, 37, 74, 119, 122, 130, 134
Hierarchy of evil 93
Hierarchy of values 93
Histoire des monastères de la Basse Egypte 145
Historia Lausiaca 145
Holy angels 145
Holy Light 122
Holy Spirit 33, 81
Holy Trinity 113, 120, 123, 124, 128, 129, 132, 135
Homo medietas 147
Horoi kai Hypographai 143

Image 29, 120
Image of God 60, 62, 99
Impassibility imperfect 127
Impassibility perfect 127
Indwelling of God 129
Inner disintegration 60
Inner restlessness 67; examples of I. R. 67ff.
Inner silence 127
Institutio ad Monachos 143
Intellect an imperishable treasure 55; only the pure I. is *capax Dei*, capable of receiving God 56; I. becomes darkened 59; I. the place of the image of God 60; I. is light 123; Intellect and "gleam of light" 129; the deified I. 131.
Intellectualism 55
Irénikon 146
Isaac of Nineveh 140

Jacob 80
Jerusalem 34
Jesus Prayer 108
Job 64, 84, 91, 114
John Cassian 22, 45–47, 77, 110, 145
John Climacus 22
John the Baptist 79
Joy 126, 128, 138

Kadloubovsky E. 143
Kellia 14, 15, 69
Kephalaia Gnôstika 143
Kierkegaard Søren 47
Kirchengeschichte Socrates of Constantinople 145
Knowledge of the heart 83; K. is "enlightenment" 124; K. of God 134, 135

Laager J. 145
Lackner W. 13.
Last thing (*eschaton*) 124
Last small step 140
Lausiac History 11, 16, 146
Lazzeri V. 141
Le Muséon 55, 107, 113, 133, 147
Les formes syriaques de la matière de l'Histoire Lausiaque 145
Lettere dal deserto 147
Letter to Melania 55
Life of prayer 77
Light 103, 122–124
Light and Darkness 31
Light of the eyes 122
Living water 35
Logos 63
Loss of spiritual sensitivity 107
Love of self (*philautia*) 61, 136, 139
Luibheid Colm 22, 145

Macarius of Alexandria 11, 69
Macarius of Egypt 96
Macarius the Great 11, 95, 108, 112
Makarios of Corinth 144
Matta al-Maskin 95
Manichaean dualism 26

Manual labor 145
Maraval 145
Master of the spiritual life 17
Maximalism 79
Maximus Confessor 136
Melania 14, 16, 23, 55, 142
Messiah 137
Meyer Robert T. 145
Minimalism 79; lukewarm M. and destructive maximalism 79
Moment of temptation 92
Monastic spirituality 21
Monastic Studies 146
Monk(s) 19, 21–23, 34, 36, 42, 48, 49, 67, 70, 71, 76–78, 92, 94, 96, 103, 112, 117, 119, 139, 140
Moore Lazarus 22
Moses 16, 118, 130, 132
Mount Sinai 118, 130
Muyldermans J. 107, 113, 115, 133, 143, 144
Mysterium iniquitatis 35
Mystical "enlightenment" 124
Myth of the devil 25

Nektarios 13
New man, born of grace 139
New Testament 34, 37
New Testament literature 37
Nikodimos of the Holy Mountain 144
Nilus of Ancyra 22
Nonnen und *Monchspiegel* [*Mirror for Monks* and *Mirror for Nuns*] 22, 143, 144
Noonday demon 46, 47, 76
Not-knowing 131, 134, 135
Nyssen W. 9, 55, 147

Obedience 14, 97, 115
Office the pre-eminent work of God 103
On Prayer 138
Origen 35, 147

Palladius 11, 12, 15, 17, 69, 73, 94, 145, 146
Palmer G.E.H. 49, 138, 143
Paradise 88

Parmentier M. 142

Parting of the ways *(Scheideweg)* 133

Pascal Blaise 47

Passion(s) 24, 26, 27, 37, 42, 43, 51, 52, 56, 57, 60, 62, 101, 121, 128, 129, 131 , 133; the double origin of all P. 53; Definition of P. 60

Passionlessness *(apatheia)* 40, 59, 63, 127

Passions of the body 43

Passions of the soul 43, 88, 90

Patience 90

Peace 126, 127, 130, 138

Peaceful state 126, 127

Pelagianism 44

Perichon 145

Perseverance 91

Person of God 28, 29, 30, 131, 136, 138

Pichery E. 145

Philokalia 143

"Philosopher in the desert" 17

Philosophy in Christian Antiquity 17

"Place of God" 128, 129, 130

Platonic philosophy 58

Praktikos 33, 69, 75, 106, 127, 144

Prayer 77, 105, 109, 118, 120, 121, 123–126, 128, 130, 138; "fiery P." 32, 110; P. of the heart 106; "one-word P." 109, 110; definition of P. 123, 125, 126; link with acedia 121

Prince of this world 24, 34

Prodigal son 137

Prudence 102, 103

Psalmodize 112

Psalmody 78, 102, 103, 111, 112

Pseudo-Supplement to the Kephalaia Gnōstika 142

Psychology of Evagrius 17

Psychosomatic phenomena 70

Pure heart 130

Quatre ermites égyptiens 146

Ramsey B. 22, 77, 145

Remembrance of death *(meletē thanatou)* 112, 137

Remembrance of God 59

Rerum monachalium rationes 144

Resurrection of the soul 124; "first or little" R. 132

Rondeau M.J. 143

Root of acedia 54

Rufinus 13, 14, 23

Rufinus Tyrannius, *Historia monachorum* 146

Russell Norman 22, 146

Sadness 53, 54, 70, 84, 88, 135

Sayings of the Fathers 17, 93

Scetis 94, 107

Schlier Heinrich 25

Schneider M. 147

Scholia in Ecclesiasten 142

Scholia in Proverbia 143

Scholia in Psalmos 143

Schulz-Flügel E. 146

Second Ecumenical Council (381) 13

Seeds of virtue 38, 43

Self-love *(philautia)* 41, 62, 81, 133, 137, 139; S. the root of all evil 72

Self-delusion 72, 74

Self-discipline 98

Secrets of the spiritual life 102

Sententiae ad Monachos 143

Sententiae ad Virgines 143

Sextus Pythagoricus 144

Sherrard Philip 49, 138, 139, 143

Sherwood Polycarp 136

Short prayers *(Stossgebete)* 108

Silouan the Athonite 29

Simplicity of heart 107

Sin 28, 42, 60, 61, 105, 129

Sinkewicz R.E. 142–145

Sins of anger 121

Sion 128

Skemmata 144

Slackness of the soul *(atonia)* 47, 89

Socrates of Constantinople 17, 145

Sorrow 85, 89

Soul 83, 113; S. the irrational part 40, 55, 87; processes within the S. 51; S. its incisive power *(thymikon)* 59; S. its intelligent power *(logistikon)* 55; S.

its desiring power *(epithymētikon)*
59; S. its passionate part 57; S. unfeel-
ing 90; S. and the governing func-
tion *(hegemonikon)* 102; the rational
S. is tripartite 58, 89, 102; S. and the
resurrection 113; S. becomes "keen-
sighted" 118; the S. and "gleam of
light" 129; S. left and right eye
123; S. impassibility 127; suffering of
the S. 61; health of the S. 59
Sozomen *Church History* 146
Spirit of despondency 106
Spirit of filiation 95
Spirit of God 95
Spiritual and simple knowledge of God
114
Spiritual death 90
Spiritual father 15–17, 94
Spiritual fatherhood 95
Spiritual indiscretion 93
Spiritual insensitivity 119
Spiritual knowledge 59
Spiritual life, one of the secrets of the S.
L. is to do all with moderation 102
Spiritual love 88
Spiritual mother 94
Spiritual motherhood 95
Spiritual teaching of Evagrius 11–19
"Spleen of Paris" 25
St Augustine 44, 134
St Paul 88, 98, 99, 127
Suarez J. M. 144
Studia Ephemeridis Augustinianum 148
Studien zum Traktat De oratione 146
Suicide 26
Synaxis 47, 78, 103
Synergia—a working together 45

Talking Back; A Monastic Handbook 142
Tears 90, 104–106, 108, 110, 125, 136
Tears of Peter 105
Temperance 88
Temptations of Christ in the Desert 41

The Greek Ascetic Corpus 143
The Mind's Long Journey to the Holy
Trinity 144
The Praktikos. Chapters on Prayer 144
Theophilos, Patriarch of Alexandria 14
Things, "letters" of God's creation 120
Thoughts of light 103, 104
Thought(s) 24, 26, 27, 37–39, 41, 42,
51–54, 57, 61, 68, 69, 71–73, 78, 81, 83,
108, 120, 121, 136; the eight T. are
generic 40; "blending or interweav-
ing of T." 56, 57
Tractatus ad Eulogium Monachum 142
Tractatus de octo spiritibus malitiae 144
Tradition of the Fathers 18
Transfer of the Spirit 96

Über die acht Gedanken 144
Unclean hearts 100

Vainglory 90
Vice 51
Vigiliae Christianae 146
Vigils 47
Vineyard of the Lord 24
Virtues 129
Vita Antonii 146
Vita Evagrii Coptice 146
Vita of Evagrius 12
Vitestam G. 142

Waiting for God 136
Ward Benedicta 18, 28
Ware Kallistos 49, 139, 143
Weariness of the heart 45
Withdrawing 114
Wimbush Vincent 143
Wisdom of the Fathers 9
Worldly people *(kosmikoi)* 48

Young elder 95

Zenos A. C. 145